8247

Library
Oakland S.U.M.

Library
Oakland S.U.M.

JUNIOR HIGH MINISTRY

Revised Edition

OTHER YOUTH SPECIALTIES BOOKS

JUNIOR HIGH

Revised Edition

MINISTRY

WAYNE RICE

ZONDERVAN PUBLISHING HOUSE
Grand Rapids, Michigan

JUNIOR HIGH MINISTRY
Copyright © 1987 by Youth Specialties, Inc.

Library of Congress Cataloging in Publication Data

Rice, Wayne.
  Junior high ministry.

  Bibliography: p.
  Includes index.
  1. Church work with adolescents. I. Title.
BV1475.9.R53 1987   259'.23   87-13335
ISBN 0-310-34970-2

All Scripture quotations, unless otherwise noted, are taken from THE HOLY BIBLE: NEW INTERNATIONAL VERSION (North American Edition). Copyright 1973, 1978, 1984 by the International Bible Society. Used by permission of Zondervan Bible Publishers.

All rights reserved. No portion of this publication may be reproduced, stored in a retrieval system, or transmitted in any form or by any means—electronic, mechanical, photocopy, recording, or by any other—except for brief quotations in printed reviews, without the prior permission of the publisher.

Edited by David Lambert

Printed in the United States of America

88 89 90 91 92 93 94 / AK / 10 9   8 7 6 5 4 3 2

Contents

Preface

Over the past twenty-three years, I have worked with junior highers in a variety of ways. I began my career in youth ministry as the junior-high director for the Youth for Christ program where I lived. Having just graduated from high school, I was given the job primarily because I didn't have enough experience to work with high-school kids. The people who hired me reasoned that I could learn about youth ministry by working with the junior-high kids, and then I could move up to "bigger and better things."

I learned, all right. I learned that (1) junior highers deserved more than inexperienced, untrained youth workers and that (2) I liked junior-high kids. That's why I've been involved with them ever since. I discovered many years ago that, contrary to popular opinion, junior highers are people too—*special* people, actually—who are at a singularly strategic point in their lives. Having made this discovery, I decided to become a junior-high specialist. I did move to the "bigger and better things" (I have worked with high schoolers), and I have had the opportunity to work with other age groups as well, but my real calling and first love continues to be junior-high ministry.

I hope that this book will help you to understand why I enjoy junior-high ministry so much. It is based largely on my personal experience, but I have attempted to reinforce my own experience with the experience of hundreds of other youth workers who have taught me a great deal over the years. I have also picked up a considerable amount of helpful information from good books and other resources dealing with early adolescence.

It has been said that one of the best ways to learn about

something is to teach it, and I have discovered this is true. Since the early seventies, I have conducted seminars on junior-high ministry as part of my work with Youth Specialties. So I have organized my thoughts on this subject as well as studied current resources and research pertinent to this age group. Many who have attended my seminars have asked that I put this information into written form. This book is the result.

This edition of *Junior High Ministry* is a complete revision of the original book, which I wrote in 1978. At first I was hesitant to make any changes, since the original book was received so well (it went through twelve printings). But times have changed and so have I. I have learned much more about junior-high ministry in the eight years that have passed, and I have also had the additional experience of being the parent of a junior higher.

As a result, I have added new material to this book and deleted some dated material. On certain issues I have tried to clarify my ideas and have even changed my mind on a few. The net result is a greatly improved book.

I must say that I have been encouraged by what has happened in junior-high ministry since the original book was written. At that time, few people took junior-high ministry seriously. It was more or less the "bad joke" of youth work. For those who did take it seriously, there were few resources to use. But that has changed. More people are getting involved in junior-high work and more quality resources are being published. Today many people would agree that the major trend in youth work at this time is an increased awareness of and commitment to junior-high ministry.

While I have tried to be thorough in this book, it is not intended to be exhaustive or the final word on junior-high ministry. Nor is it intended to replace any of the fine books currently available on adolescent psychology and youth ministry. It is a look at junior-high ministry from one veteran's point of view; I only hope that it will complement the work of others. It covers most of the basics, as I see them, and is designed to stimulate and to challenge both the experienced and the inexperienced junior-high worker in the Christian community. Of course, my greatest hope is that a lot of junior-high kids will benefit.

For the purpose of this book, I have defined a junior higher as any young person between the ages of eleven and fourteen. Usually that means the seventh, eighth, and ninth grades, but this material is not limited either to those ages or to those years in school. We can give or take a year or two on either side and still be talking about the same group of kids.

In this book, I refer to these young people most of the time as "junior highers," although I frequently use the term "early adolescents," which is more common in the academic community. Occasionally I call them "kids." Some people may object because they think this sounds too young for this age group, but I have found that most junior highers use this term to refer to themselves. "Students" is another term I sometimes use; it has a nice neutral ring to it.

It is interesting, by the way, that there really isn't a name for this group that is exclusively theirs. There is no term that adequately identifies the eleven- to fourteen-year-old except those that imply they are "not quite" something else. The term *junior higher* actually means that they are "not quite" high schoolers; *early adolescent* means that they are "not quite" adolescents. In the book *The Vanishing Adolescent*, Edgar Friedenberg says that if a society has no word for something, either it does not matter to them, or it scares them to talk about it. Maybe we need to come up with a better name for our eleven- to fourteen-year-olds. Any ideas?

Another problem that has arisen in recent years to complicate the lives of people who try to write clear sentences is the controversy over the use of the sexist pronouns *he* and *she*. I share people's objections to using the masculine *he* or *him* when also referring to *she* or *her*, but I have a greater distaste for constantly using "he or she" throughout a book. I have used "he or she" when I felt it sounded better to do so, but most of the time I have used the traditional "he" to indicate both masculine and feminine. Hopefully, you can add your own "or she" in those cases, with my apologies.

I would like to take this opportunity to express my thanks to some people who have been very helpful and supportive to me over the years. At Youth Specialties, I am privileged to keep company with some of the finest people in the world: Mike Yaconelli, Tic Long, Noel Becchetti, Bill McNabb, Jim Burns, Rich Van Pelt, Duffy Robbins, and many other good friends who have helped me sharpen my youth ministry skills. In addition, I am indebted to the dozens of other junior-high workers who have inspired me over the years and have allowed me to "pick their brains" from time to time, especially Bill Wennerholm, who was one of the first. I really appreciate all of these quality people from whom I have learned a lot. I want to express gratitude to Joan Lipsitz and everyone at the Center for Early Adolescence in Carrboro, North Carolina, for all their outstanding work. They have been a tremendous resource for me.

I also want to thank my editor at Zondervan Publishing House, Dave Lambert, for all his work on this book. And thanks again to Bob DeVries for encouraging me to write the original version back when I didn't think I could write at all. I still feel that way most of the time, but now I don't worry about it so much.

My wife Marci never complained, even though I took up a lot of "our" time working on this revision. Fortunately, she loves junior-high kids as much as I do, especially those who live in our house. Thanks to my kids, Nathan, Amber, and Corey, who often tried to tear their dad away from the word processor long enough for him to do things dads are supposed to do. Again, I'll take this opportunity to say to my family: "I love you."

Part I

JUNIOR-HIGH MINISTRY AND YOU

1.
JUNIOR-HIGH MINISTRY IN THE LOCAL CHURCH

This book is about young adolescents who are approximately eleven through fourteen years old. They are referred to as "junior highers" primarily because of the educational institutions that most of this age group attend—junior high schools. Of course, age is seldom an accurate means for isolating a group of people into a category, but we do so with this group because society, through such institutions as junior high and middle schools, recognizes the years eleven through fourteen as a separate stage of life. And rightly so. Early adolescence is a singularly special time of a person's life. But simply categorizing them is not enough. While junior highers have been labeled as a "stage," they have also become one of the most neglected groups of people in today's society. As one twelve-year-old girl wrote, "Grown ups don't think you're very important if you are over 10 and under 14. But if you're younger than 10 and older than 14, then you're important. When I was 11, I thought I was important, but after the first couple of months I found out that I'm just a plain old boring kid."

My objective in this book is to show that this age group is indeed important and to suggest some practical ways for the Christian church to reverse the trend of neglect and to minister to junior highers more effectively. It is my conviction that ministry to junior-high students, people between the ages of eleven and fourteen, is without a doubt one of the most important and strategic ministries for the church. Hopefully, this book will help you—the pastor, the youth director, the volunteer—to catch this vision and to understand better how to meet the needs of early adolescents.

Usually when youth ministry is considered in the church, the primary concern is with high-school students or with the college group, even though there may be more junior highers. It is not uncommon for a church to spend a substantial amount of money on programing and professional staff to meet the needs of senior highers without ever considering the same for its junior highers. The children's department of the church naturally concerns itself only with children up through the sixth grade, since the seventh grader is viewed as having outgrown all the old methods and is now ready for something else. The problem is that few people seem to know what that something else is. So the end result is that the junior higher is more often than not put on hold; we wait for him to pass through this stage and to grow up into someone to whom we are better equipped to minister.

There are many reasons why junior highers have been traditionally neglected in the church. Perhaps the most obvious one is that the vast majority of adults are afraid of junior-high kids. Adults seem to be intimidated by junior highers or at least to have an acute distaste for them. Most parents I know would be delighted if somehow their own kids were able to by-pass the junior-high years altogether.

Adults don't feel this way about older teenagers or younger children. Senior highers appear to be, in many ways, a lot like young adults. They are somewhat predictable and are able to communicate on a more mature level. They can drive, have money, and are often willing to work and to take on many leadership responsibilities—all of which makes the youth worker's job a great deal easier. Junior highers generally offer none of the above, and this unfortunately discourages many people from getting involved in junior-high ministry.

Similarly, the prospect of working with or teaching the younger children in the church poses no real threat or problem for the adult who wishes to serve in some way. To the youngster, the adult represents authority, knowledge, power, and deserves re-spect. Most adults enjoy this kind of recognition. Little kids are, for the most part, manageable, cute, and, on top of that, believe most everything you tell them. Not so with junior highers. Much to everyone's dismay, they love to challenge authority, and they have a knack for asking disturbing questions that are often difficult, if not impossible, to answer.

According to Don Wells, principal of the Carolina Friends School and member of the Task Force on Middle Schools (National Association of Independent Schools), junior highers are neglected by adults for the following reasons:

1) Early adolescents defy being defined, and that's irritating. We can set some hazy marks about them on a scale relative to any act, value, skill, or any other single thing, but the result is either as useful as a definitive description of all bubbles, or so definitive as to classify all bubbles, save one, the exception. And those things we can't define, can't make sound predictions about, indeed those things that even resist our efforts to classify them by the effrontery of simply being themselves, we tend to avoid. In the case of the early adolescent, we have avoided.

2) Because of our inability to define, the holder of the needed information is a child, and what adult wants to be dependent on a *child* as his resource person? Precious few it seems.

3) The number of persons who had a positive, healthy, happy early adolescence in a supportive, caring environment equals the number of adults presently whole enough to creatively and maturely identify with an early adolescent toward the goal of successful interaction. Such persons were an endangered species long before the blue whale.

4) We all have fragile egos, and we all play to the audience "out there." When we have our druthers, we pick good audiences because they tend to make us feel good. Early adolescents are very unpredictable audiences, and many times they hiss and boo. Not because they don't like you, but because they aren't sure they like themselves; not because they want to corporately hurt you, but because they aren't thinking corporately but individually; not because they understand and reject, but because they don't understand that you don't understand.

5) To appreciate the world of the early adolescent, one must "become" in the world of the early adolescent. Such total immersion is not as necessary when working with other age groups, for we readily accept that we can never experience early childhood again and we delight in our ability to enjoy, nurture, and support the childhood experience. Also, we revel in the fact that we can have "adult dialogue" with children beyond early adolescence, and although we then have to take full cognizance of their burgeoning physical and mental prowess, they do seem eminently more reasonable than they were just a few years back. Early adolescence cannot be dealt with so neatly, for it has been the stage in our lives replete with terror, anxiety, fear, loneliness, hate, love, joy, desperation, all expressed (or experienced) with the intensity

of adulthood yet devoid of adult perspective. It is an age of vulnerability, and vulnerability implies potential pain; adults know that pain
hurts, and they don't often willingly enter a domain in which they will
be hurt. So we avoid (deny) because we as adults cannot again handle
adolescence.

6) Early adolescents are easily identifiable as imperfect specimens of the
human condition. They are not the epitome of anything we can define
as "good" from our adult perspective. Since they aren't consistent, they
can't reach perfection on our terms. We don't use positive superlatives
in describing them. All of us, however, generally prefer dealing with
those who have "made it" in the superlative sense. Therefore, because
early adolescents are moving in such constant flux, they never make it
to a desirous end within that stage. Dealing with early adolescents does
not afford us the satisfaction of experiencing a finished product, and we
lose vision and perspective easily. (And so do they.)[1]

In other words, most people avoid junior-high ministry
because most people avoid things that appear to be unpleasant.
People don't usually stand in line to sign up for a bad time. Junior
highers are stereotyped as being rowdy, restless, silly, impossible to
handle, moody, vulgar, disrespectful, and worst of all, unpredictable. Unfortunately, all of these characteristics may be true at
times, but to be completely fair, the truth is that junior highers
offer more than enough to offset whatever hazards may exist in
working with them. They are, for example, tremendously enthusiastic, fun, loyal, energetic, open, and, most importantly, ready to
learn just as much as the creative youth worker is willing to help
them learn. The personal satisfaction and sense of accomplishment
that are part of working with junior highers are unequaled
anywhere else.

I have served in several churches and parachurch organizations in a variety of roles, and I have had the opportunity to work
with most age groups. I've run "children's church," organized
summer camps, led Bible studies, preached a few sermons, led
worship services, and much more. I have to be honest and say that
I probably enjoy most working with people closer to my own age. I
am, after all, an adult, and I can identify in more ways with adults
than with kids. But having said that, I can also say with an equal
degree of certainty that if I were to select the most challenging and
rewarding area of ministry in the church, it would have to be
working with junior-high kids.

Most people believe that the most important job in the church belongs to the senior pastor, or the person who works with the adults. Possibly—but consider this: In most cases, the pastor works with people who have already made decisions about everything important in their lives. They have already decided upon their careers, lifestyles, value systems, husbands and wives, and religious beliefs. The junior-high worker, on the other hand, works with people who still have all those important decisions in front of them. Unlike the pastor who works primarily with adults, the junior-high worker gets to influence all those decisions before they are made. Maybe we underestimate just how important junior-high ministry is in the church.

I have on a number of occasions heard intelligent people comment that all one can really expect to do is more or less "baby-sit" junior highers until they get older. Just keep an eye on them, give them enough activity to hold their attention, and wait until they "grow up." They just aren't mature enough for any kind of "meaningful" ministry now, they say. To expend a great deal of effort working with junior highers is like throwing pearls before swine. It is better stewardship of both time and money to wait until you can really do some good. Wait until they reach high school.

My answer to that is a story: There was a pathway that ended abruptly at the edge of a high cliff, and for some unknown reason, day after day people would walk off the end of the pathway without stopping and fall off the cliff onto the jagged rocks below. After years of losing citizens to this problem, the local authorities finally decided to do something about it. So they brought in a team of experts to assess the situation and to make some recommendations. After much study and discussion, the experts decided that the best thing to do would be to build a hospital at the bottom of the cliff!

What makes this story so silly is that the problem is not at the bottom of the cliff, but at the top. Anyone can see that what needs to be done is to find some way to keep people from falling off the cliff. I believe that junior highers stand precisely at the top of the cliff. To wait until they are "older" is like building a hospital at the bottom of the cliff. Junior highers need help now, not later. If we wait until they are older, we may not get the opportunity to help them. Most surveys I have seen indicate that the person most likely to drop out of church is a ninth grader. It is during the junior-high years that many young people decide that they are tired of being baby-sat.

A TIME OF TRANSITION

I read a story in the newspaper recently about a European traveler who wanted to get to Oakland, California. He bought a ticket in Frankfurt, Germany, to Los Angeles International Airport, with a connecting flight to Oakland. When he arrived in Los Angeles, he asked someone at the ticket counter where the flight to Oakland could be boarded. Because of the traveler's poor English, the person at the counter thought he said "Auckland." Incredibly, the traveler mistakenly wound up on a plane to Auckland, New Zealand, instead of Oakland, California, and fifteen hours later found himself halfway around the world in a country he had no desire to visit at all.

Perhaps the moral of the story is this: *Watch your connections.* Changes can be very important, not only in airports, but in life. And of course, some of the biggest changes in life take place during the junior-high years.

The years between eleven and fifteen are without a doubt the most unsettling in a person's life. This is when puberty occurs, when a person changes physically from a child to an adult. But there are many other changes as well. During this period there is a tremendous amount of upheaval, which takes many different forms. This once-in-a-lifetime metamorphosis and most of the resulting changes will be discussed in greater detail later in this book.

Misconceptions often abound regarding puberty. It is not a disease, so it doesn't need a cure. Everyone experiences it, so it's perfectly normal, even though it results in what appears to be abnormal behavior.

For example, it is not uncommon for a junior higher to catch a sudden case of the giggles or to erupt into tears without warning. Or he might be bursting with energy one moment, yet for no apparent reason become lethargic and lazy the next. He will sometimes act very much like an adult and at other times act like a child. He may become unusually preoccupied with the mirror and worry to the point of depression about every supposed defect in his physical appearance. He may decide to do something one moment and then immediately change his mind and do precisely the opposite—hardly what one would call "normal" behavior. Actually when working with junior highers, it is a good idea to keep in mind that the abnormal *is* normal most of the time.

For some junior highers, the new experiences and problems they encounter during puberty will be mild and go practically unnoticed by the casual observer. But for most kids, puberty provides serious difficulty, and often they suffer from a complete inability to cope. Erik Erikson writes that it is not until adolescence that the individual begins to see himself as having a past and a future that are exclusively his. Early adolescence is thus a pivotal time of review and anticipation.[2] It is during these years that the child attempts to "put away childish things" in his quest to become a person with a unique identity, and most of the time these efforts result in a lot of frustration, even failure. As the junior higher begins to break away from parental domination, to seek autonomy and a degree of independence, complications arise. Parents are naturally reluctant to let go, and they often don't understand what is going on. Meanwhile, the kids are certain that they are not being allowed to grow up and that the only possible solution is to rebel.

During the junior-high years the juvenile crime rate soars. There is much in the news these days about teenage runaways, teenage drug abusers, teenage pregnancy, and teenage suicide, and much of that news is about young people under the age of fifteen. Without belaboring the point, there is more than enough evidence to show that the junior-high years are uniquely troublesome and require more, not less, of the church's concern and attention.

It is both ironic and tragic that the reality of "transition" in junior highers is also one of the primary reasons that junior highers are neglected. There are those who would say that since junior highers are "in transition"—neither one thing nor the other ("in-between-agers")—then the best thing we can do is to "wait for them to grow out of it." Wait for them to settle down. In other

19

words, trying to minister effectively to junior highers is akin to trying to hit a moving target.

But they don't "grow out of it." The changes that take place during early adolescence, and the supervision and guidance (or lack of it) that they receive during this time, leave an indelible mark on their lives far into adulthood. The experiences of early adolescence are life shaping and life changing. As Erikson says, "the growth events of adolescence are in large measure determined by what has happened before and *they determine much of what follows* [italics mine]."[3] This is why early adolescence occupies such a pivotal position in a person's life.

A TIME OF QUESTIONING

At this age, the mind is also developing rapidly, so most junior highers begin to call into question much of what they have been taught. Many childhood myths crumble as they discover new ways of perceiving reality. They no longer consider everything their parents or teachers tell them to be true; they want to understand for themselves.

One fourteen-year-old girl describes the conflict between her old and new perspective. "I had a whole philosophy of how the world worked. I was very religious and I believed that there was unity and harmony and that everything had its proper place. I used to imagine rocks in the right places on all the right beaches. It was all very neat and God ordained it all, but now it seems absolutely ridiculous."[4]

It is not at all uncommon for junior highers to suspend temporarily or even to reject entirely the values and beliefs acquired during childhood. This questioning continues until they are able to determine whether these values and beliefs have any validity for or relevance to their new young adult lives. Just as Santa Claus and the stork were discarded years earlier, so the God of the Old Testament and the Christ of the New Testament seem not quite as believable as they once were.

In light of this, it would seem obvious that it is foolish for the church merely to occupy junior highers with meaningless activity rather than offer them thoughtful and honest answers to the questions that issue out of their emerging faith. There is certainly a danger here of losing them entirely with little chance of reclaiming them later.

A TIME OF OPENNESS

One of the primary reasons that working with junior highers can be unusually strategic is that young adolescents are very open to new ideas and to guidance. For most junior highers, their search for an identity is a complicated trial-and-error process, which accounts for their characteristic unpredictability. They will accept or try things one day that they might discard the next for something completely different. They will act out a particular role or behave in a particular way that coincides with their concept of how they want to be and how they want others to view them until they have a pretty good idea of how others will respond. If they are dissatisfied with the feedback they receive, they will more than likely discontinue this behavior and seek out some other alternative. This is why a junior higher's entire personality can change from one week to the next; for example, the things he wanted to do last week he no longer wants to do this week. Such behavior is all part of an important growing-up process. For the junior higher, life is like a big jigsaw puzzle with a lot of the pieces missing. His job is to find all the pieces and put them into place.

Senior-high students, by comparison, are nearing the completion of this process and will often be extremely rigid and set in their ways. Normally, by the time teenagers graduate from high school, they have already adopted the personality, lifestyle, and values that will be theirs for the rest of their lives. This is why it is so easy to make accurate predictions about seniors.

I remember attending my ten-year class reunion, which brought together most of the class of '63. It was good to see my old friends and classmates once again, but it was also kind of eerie. I had the strange feeling all evening that I had been put into a time machine as I renewed old acquaintances and watched the action on the dance floor. It was like being back in high school all over again because everyone was so much the same. I discovered that, with few exceptions, I could have made very accurate predictions in

21

1963 as to what those high school graduates would be like ten years down the road. The introverts were still introverts; the extroverts had become insurance salesmen or politicians; the high achievers had become successful in business or in education; the class "flakes" were still flakes.

This is in stark contrast to the openness, flexibility, and unpredictability of the junior higher. Trying to pin them down is like trying to nail Jell-O to a wall. They remain open to all kinds of possibilities for their lives.

Of course, this openness often takes the form of gullibility. They are not always the most discriminating people in the world and will try almost anything, at least once. This is why new fads are so popular with junior highers. Everybody has got to try it. The junior higher is an easy target for Madison Avenue, the rock-and-roll disc jockey, the drug pusher, or anyone selling just about anything. They know who is going to buy their product.

The church has just as much potential as the world to capture the attention of this age group. Kids are open not only to fads and bad influences; they are also open to positive guidance and direction for their lives. It is doubtful that there will ever again be a better or more strategic time to reach young people for Jesus Christ.

A TIME OF DECISION

A recent survey of more than 8,000 early adolescents revealed that the *value* that increases the most between the 5th and the 9th grades is "to make my own decisions."[5] As junior highers approach adulthood, they covet the one major characteristic of adulthood that has until now been withheld from them: the ability to make their own decisions. While they were children, parents, guardians, and other authority figures made all of their important decisions for them. But now they want the right to begin making these decisions for themselves. This does not mean that junior highers want to be *independent*. Actually, what they want is *autonomy*, the ability to make decisions about things that are important to them. They want to decide who their friends will be, what clothes they will wear, what music they will listen to, and so on. Likewise, they are anxious to make decisions about their values, faith, and other commitments. Their quest for autonomy pushes them to make as many of the decisions that govern their lives as possible.

Most people agree that junior highers do not make *lasting* decisions. Erik Erikson maintains that early adolescents between the ages of eleven and fifteen are not ready to "install lasting idols or ideals as guardians of a final identity."[6] It is true that most junior highers are engaged in a fact-finding period that makes the majority of their assumptions, conclusions, and decisions rather fragile and temporary. But for some junior highers, significant decisions are possible, and they may have considerable impact upon them for the rest of their lives. The late novelist Ayn Rand claims that she "decided" to become an atheist at thirteen. And of course, I'm sure you can point to those people, as can I, who claim to have made a commitment to Christ during their early adolescent years.

What can we say about decisions like that? Simply that the decision-making process begins (or at least gains impetus) during early adolescence, and that some of these decisions will receive enough confirmation and support in the years that follow to last.

Junior highers have reached a very important crossroad. They are now ready to take some responsibility for their lives. They can begin making good decisions or bad ones. I believe that it is our job in junior-high ministry not to try to get that "final" decision. We need to teach junior highers how to make good decisions, how to exercise good judgment, and how to understand the consequences of their decisions. And we need to give junior highers the freedom to make decisions on their own without coercion or manipulation on our part. If their decisions are going to have any meaning at all, they must come as a result of their own reasoning, understanding, and process of elimination.

The temptation for the Christian junior-high worker is to push for decisions—ask junior highers to make a commitment to follow Christ, to be a good witness for Christ, and the like. And usually the decision can't wait, it must be made immediately. ("Now is the accepted time," we tell them.) Of course, if the case for such a commitment has been communicated in an appealing way, it is likely that the junior-high worker will get good results. Junior highers will usually make just as many decisions as they are asked to make. Like I said earlier, they will try almost anything, once.

The problem is that spiritual decisions like these are taken very seriously in the church and are considered to be of a sacred, life-changing nature. Yet, for the young adolescent who has been put on the spot and asked to make a decision before he was ready, it has become just one more decision.

In Scripture, commitment to Christ is compared to a marriage. It's for life. Christ is the bridegroom; we are the bride. We would not give a junior-high marriage much chance of success, but we often push junior highers to make a final decision about their faith that is equal in importance to a marriage vow.

I have seen posters in youth group meeting rooms that said "Not to decide is to decide." This is a catchy phrase and very motivating, but it also creates a real problem for junior highers. There are many times when not to decide is the best thing they can do. Junior highers need the church's help as they attempt to gain a better understanding of the implications of the Christian commitment, but they do not need to be pushed into making a premature commitment. It is unfortunate that many young people are decisioned to death in the church during those junior-high years, which makes a lasting commitment less likely later in life.

It is not our job as junior-high workers to produce a large number of decisions. More times than not we fall into that trap only because we want some kind of measurable results; we want to know how we are doing. They are more for our good than anyone else's. Significant decisions will be made along the way by junior highers, but it is wiser to teach the kids how to make good decisions and to allow their decisions to come on their own.

A TIME FOR ATTENTION

A generation ago, "youth ministry" was virtually synonymous with "high-school ministry." All of the major Christian youth movements, such as Youth for Christ and Young Life, were aimed at high-school teenagers. Junior highers were still considered "children." But times have changed. In the words of Dr. Urie Bronfenbrenner of Cornell University, "the adolescents today are

24

the twelve-year-olds, and the eleven-year-olds, and the ten-year-olds. That is, they are having the experiences that five years earlier, adolescents didn't have until they were 13, 14, and 15; and they, in turn, are having the experiences that adolescents used to have when they were 16, 17, and 18."[7]

Today, the "cutting edge" of youth ministry will be found in the junior high and middle school. Certainly high-school ministry remains very important, perhaps even more so than before, but more and more youth workers are discovering that if youth ministry is to be taken seriously, then junior highers must also be taken seriously.

Dr. Gary Downing, an adolescent psychologist who has also worked with teenagers for many years, says it well:

> Because early adolescent growth has accelerated so much over the last twenty years . . . we must rethink our assumptions, our strategies, and our programs in order to respond to the changing needs of kids. We must overcome our ignorance, apathy, and our stereotypes so that we do not lose a whole generation of people so desperately in need of our love and concern. We cannot afford to dismiss this young subculture as "too squirrelly, too energetic, too disrespectful, or too shallow" to be worthy of our time and resources. We cannot expect to "warehouse" this group for several years and expect that they will be waiting for us when we decide we are ready for them. They won't be there tomorrow because we aren't here today when they need us the most.[8]

The junior-high years offer us a unique opportunity for ministry in the local church. At no other time in a person's life are so many options considered, changes made, and lives shaped. It is not a time for baby-sitting but for loving attention. We need to let every junior higher we encounter know that he is significant to Christ, to the church, and to the world around him. Young minds and growing faiths have many questions that require honest answers from caring adults. These kids are attempting to establish themselves as individuals worthy of the love of God.

2.
THE JUNIOR-HIGH WORKER

A friend of mine who has been involved in full-time junior-high ministry for almost twenty years once told me, "If you can learn how to run a junior-high group, then you can rule the world." Whether or not you take him seriously, the point he was trying to make is a good one: It does take a special kind of person to work with junior-high kids. If you are willing to develop the skills, patience, courage, and know-how required to work with junior highers, then anything else you want to do later ought to be a breeze (including ruling the world, should you be so inclined).

The importance of the person who chooses to be a junior-high worker should not be underestimated. The junior-high worker or teacher is central to the success or failure of any program or methodology. Junior-high work is essentially relational, and the people involved in it are the main ingredient.

There is an abundance of good resources, ideas, curriculum and books available for junior-high programs (believe it or not), but the truth is that if the kids don't like or can't relate to the teacher/sponsor/youth worker in charge, then there is little chance that anything will work very well. The good news is that the reverse is also true most of the time. That is, if you are the kind of person who relates well to junior highers and if you are able to communicate with them reasonably well, then it's likely that you could use almost any resource or new idea successfully. This, of course, doesn't mean that the junior-high worker who relates well to junior highers doesn't have to be selective about resources, but he or she does have a distinct advantage.

Junior highers nearly always describe their youth programs or classes in terms of the youth worker or teacher. *They* are the ones who make the class or program great or terrible. It is interesting that high-school and college students almost always select their classes by subject after they have looked over the course offerings. But with junior highers, there is little concern about content. The important question from one junior higher to the other is always, "*Who* did you get?" The goal is to get the good teachers and to avoid the bad ones.

Educator Edward Martin comments about attempts to separate the teaching from the teacher:

> Curriculum reform projects of the past ten years in the academic disciplines have tried to improve schools by producing better materials, some of which could be taught by any teacher. Most of them now realize that with a bad teacher, students will feel the new course is as bad as the old. Parents, principals, and guidance counselors keep telling youngsters that it should not matter who the teacher is. They say you should be able to learn from someone you do not like. This is true only when the personal dislike is mild and is overpowered by respect for the teacher's fairness and competence.[1]

It would be convenient if everyone who was willing or available could do the job, but unfortunately, there are people who just can't be junior-high workers. They don't have the right characteristics. And that means that if we in the church really care about meeting the needs of our junior highers, then we should make every effort to have qualified people working with them.

And what is a qualified person?

First, a word about some "unqualifications." Take, for example, the stereotype of the typical junior-high worker: a handsome, young, funny, athletic, single college student who plays a guitar, owns a custom-built van with a stereo in the back, and has an apartment at the beach. Even with all these "assets," this person could be hopelessly unqualified to work with junior highers. It is possible, of course, to win the affection and admiration of junior highers for a while by being cool or by having musical ability, good looks, and the latest clothing styles, but most good junior-high workers that I know possess few of these. That doesn't mean you cannot be young, beautiful, and talented, but you certainly don't have to be in order to relate well and minister effectively to junior highers. Sometimes those "positive" assets can actually be a hindrance if kids perceive that you "have it all together" and they don't. They may feel threatened by you unless you let them know that you have faults and imperfections just like they do. Kids will like you and listen to you not because you happen to be "neat" or glamorous, but because you like them and listen to them.

Now on to the qualifications.

One prerequisite for working with junior highers (or any age group for that matter) in the church is spiritual maturity. I assume that anyone who takes on a position of leadership in the church has a meaningful relationship with Christ that can be communicated to others. This does not mean, of course, that a junior-high worker must be a spiritual giant; it does mean that he or she should have a faith that is alive and growing. It is inappropriate for someone who does not have this basic foundation to teach or otherwise minister to others in the church.

At a workshop on junior-high ministry a few years ago, a group of overzealous youth workers brainstormed a list of "characteristics of an effective junior-high worker" and came up with twenty-seven different items. Just looking at that list made me feel discouraged. Since the "perfect" junior-high worker doesn't exist, I'll spare you those twenty-seven characteristics. Instead, I'll narrow it down to the six I consider the most important.

1. You must be able to identify with the problems, needs, and feelings of junior highers.
2. You must like junior highers.
3. You must have patience.
4. You must be a good listener.
5. You must have a positive attitude and a sense of humor.
6. You must be willing and able to give the necessary time.

Most of these qualifications can be learned. People do not naturally possess a liking for junior highers or good listening skills, but they can be acquired. Few junior-high workers will score high on all six of the above characteristics; for example, it's possible to be a good junior-high worker and be a little short of patience or lack a sharp sense of humor. On the other hand, it would be safe to say that a person who flunks out on any one of these six areas is going to encounter some real difficulty relating and ministering to junior highers.

LEARNING TO UNDERSTAND THEM

The first qualification for a junior-high worker is the ability to identify with the early adolescent, that is, to understand what it is like to be a junior-high person. Most adults just can't do it. To most adults, junior highers seem incredibly strange and impossible to understand. They are moody, noisy, unreasonable, disrespectful, irreverent, lazy, and just plain crazy most of the time, Mr. Average Adult would say. And of course, to the casual observer, most of these things are more or less true. But to the junior higher, there are very good reasons behind all those idiosyncrasies that adults don't like, and junior highers desperately want someone who will try to understand. Without this understanding, communication becomes almost impossible.

Every adult has one very good point of identification with junior highers—he or she was once upon a time a junior higher, too. You and I were junior-high kids not *too* many years ago. Even though the world that today's junior highers are growing up in has changed, most of the problems that they face today are not that different from the problems we faced when we were their age. It would seem, then, that we should naturally have a certain amount of empathy because we do have something in common.

But psychologists tell us that there is a problem for normal adults when it comes to remembering what it was like to be an adolescent between the ages of eleven and fourteen. They call it "repression," which is a kind of adult amnesia. Repression is defined as the "rejection from consciousness of painful or disagreeable ideas, memories, and feelings." To make life more endurable, the mind automatically tries to forget, or at least block from memory, painful past experiences. Those painful experiences are never lost completely from consciousness; they are just pushed back into the recesses of the mind and never recalled. It's common for therapists to use hypnosis or some other method to help people recall and deal with repressed events.

What does all this have to do with our working with junior highers? Simply that psychologists tell us that some of life's most painful experiences have occurred to us during puberty, when we were junior highers. Consider the embarrassment and humiliation of having to dress for that first P.E. class; the struggle with parents

29

for independence; the times when you were not accepted into the right group of kids; guilt feelings brought on by new awareness of your sexuality; puzzling questions from a developing mind; love triangles and broken hearts; and the list could go on and on. No one wants to go through life with all *that* on his mind, so it is repressed. And that accounts for the average adult's inability to understand junior highers very well. They just don't remember. Says educator John A. Rice:

> . . . but where is one who does not wince at the memory of his adolescence? . . . Women say they cannot remember the pangs of childbirth. Crafty nature blots them, lest there be no more children. So also one does not remember one's second birth . . . from childhood into youth. This second birth . . . becomes in memory a dull pain.[2]

The best way for you to identify with junior highers is to get in touch with your own early adolescent years. Sure, it's hard to reach back and relive events and recall feelings from a long time ago, but it isn't impossible and it does wonders to help you empathize with kids. Understanding junior highers does not mean that you need to be an expert on youth or youth culture; it just means that you need to develop a good memory. Your memory can be one of your greatest resources as a junior-high worker. There have been many occasions when I have looked into the face of a twelve- or thirteen-year-old who was having a problem of one kind or another and felt for a moment like I was looking into a mirror. I recognized myself as a boy around that age. That realization helped me tremendously as I listened to him and attempted to relate to him and offer guidance.

If your memory and you cannot cooperate, it's not likely that you will need to go to a psychiatrist or a hypnotist for therapy. Sometimes just being around junior highers a lot will do the trick. You might talk to people who knew you well when you were a junior higher (like your parents, if possible). Sometimes it's helpful just to try to write down as much as you can remember about those years. In my office, I have a picture of myself when I was in the eighth grade. It's a constant reminder to myself that I was once a junior-high kid.

Regardless of whether you are able to recall instantly your youth, it is wise to read as many books and articles on adolescent psychology as you can. Check your public library. The chapters in this book dealing with the characteristics of junior highers will hopefully be helpful to you as well, and I have listed other resources for further reading in the back of this book. Doing some homework is an excellent way not only to stay informed but also to jolt the memory when remembering does not come easy.

Keep in mind that the reason for all this remembering and reading is to bring about a better understanding of junior highers and an identification with their problems and feelings. Without this, it becomes very difficult to meet the demands of being a junior-high worker. Young adolescents often appear to exaggerate their miseries and to overdramatize their suffering, and it's hard to be very supportive when deep down we just don't believe things are as bad as they let on. And, of course, its entirely possible that they may not be. But to the junior higher, his suffering is very real, and adult advice, criticism, and analysis is the last thing he needs in a moment of crisis. When a person is hurting, he needs a soothing balm, some encouragement, a shoulder to cry on, someone who will listen and understand. When a junior higher tells you that he or she is the ugliest person in his or her peer group, believe it. You have been given an important piece of information. Your acceptance must come first; advice, reason, and perspective can come later.

Like many kids going through puberty, I had my share of romantic experiences when I was in junior-high school. Whenever I would fall in love with the girl who sat on the other side of the classroom, or with the pastor's daughter, or whoever the lucky girl happened to be at the time, I was certain that it was the real thing. Someday we would be married, have kids, and live happily ever after. But the adults in my life, parents especially, would only smile and to my great dismay classify it as puppy love. I can't describe how much pain that caused. In retrospect, they were right: It *was* puppy love. But puppy love is very real to puppies.

LEARNING TO LIKE THEM

A few years ago I conducted a survey of some seven hundred junior-high kids from all over the United States, and I asked each young person to answer a number of questions. One of the questions was "If you could ask any question and get a straight answer, what would it be?"

Naturally, I received many different responses, but there was one that appeared more than all the others. It seems that the question on the minds of many, if not most, junior highers is simply "Do you like me?"

They want to know if they are liked and accepted. They aren't concerned about the theological issues of the day, or about how they can be better Christians at school, or what the future holds. The real issue that gets top priority with so many junior highers today is "Am I O.K.? Do you like me?"

More recent studies conducted by Search Institute have shown that not being liked is ranked among the top three worries of early adolescents, even ahead of nuclear war and death.[3] Being accepted is very important to a junior higher, and more often than not, they will pledge absolute loyalty to whoever gives that acceptance to them. Like nearly everyone else, they like to be liked, but their insecurities give this need a greater significance. Their need to be liked is linked closely with their emerging adulthood and their quest for independence. They are not certain whether they are *likable,* which they perceive to be an important prerequisite for success in the adult world.

The implications for junior-high workers should be obvious. A good junior-high worker is one who genuinely likes junior-high kids—a necessity for anyone hoping for a meaningful and productive ministry with junior highers. Understanding is important, but unless you like to be around them, understanding becomes merely an academic exercise. There are many experts in the field of early adolescence who have never developed a liking for the young people they know so much about. I have asked numerous junior-high principals to name the most important characteristic of a good junior-high teacher, and the one most often mentioned is "They've got to like junior-high kids."

There are degrees of liking, of course. You may be one who likes junior highers a great deal or only mildly (that's okay), but the important thing is that what you have comes through for the kids to see. It's not enough to simply announce "I like you" now and then and leave it at that. Words rarely make a good substitute for actions. Junior highers need to see words translated into actions. *Show* them that you really like them whenever you can.

Practically speaking, this means that you should try to develop friendships with kids individually. Learn their names—well. I have discovered the hard way that forgetting a junior higher's name can be extremely destructive to a developing relationship. Find out each one's likes and dislikes, interests, and concerns. Visit their homes, meet their parents and learn their family situations. Sometimes the best way to get to know a junior higher is to get a guided tour of his or her bedroom. You can learn a lot by looking at all the posters and other paraphernalia on the walls and shelves.

I have found that one of the best ways to show junior highers that you really like them is to do things with them that are not required of you. After all, they know that you are going to be involved with them in planning programs and meetings, teaching classes, and even visiting them on occasion because it's your job. That's what you are expected to do as a youth-group leader. But when you are willing to give up some of your own free time to be with them, that's different. Only a friend would do that.

Perhaps you could take a few kids on a fishing, camping, or backpacking trip, or invite some of them (even on short notice) to a ball game or movie some evening. Try taking kids shopping with you on a Saturday afternoon, or inviting them to your home during the week, or hosting a slumber party. These are all good ways to let kids know that you enjoy their company.

When I was in junior-high school, my family went to a small church that didn't have much of a youth program except for a Sunday night youth meeting just before the evening service. Our pastor's younger brother, Jerry, was given the responsibility of leading those youth group meetings for several years. Today, I can't recall much of what happened at any of those Sunday night meetings of almost thirty years ago, but I'll never forget Jerry. I remember well that every Saturday Jerry would come around in his car and pick up several of us boys and we would shoot baskets, or go bowling, or head for the beach, or just mess around. As a junior higher, I considered him one of my best friends, even though he was a lot older than I, and I know I would have done almost anything for Jerry. During those years when I was having a great deal of trouble finding acceptance from adults and being treated like a real person, Jerry liked me and was my friend. That was more important than great youth meetings. I am certain now that Jerry played a big role in my development both as a person and as a Christian.

Anytime you can give personal attention to your junior highers, you are going to be letting them know that you are serious when you say that you care about them. Sometimes all it takes is a phone call during the week reminding them of something, thanking them for something, asking a favor of them, or just checking up on how they are doing. Calling someone for no particular reason is something that a *friend* would do. I have used the mail in much the same way. Junior highers love to get mail, and a personal, affirming note now and then helps tremendously to show kids that you think of them more than on Sundays only.

Keep in mind through all this that if you are an adult, you need to retain your identity and not try to give the impression that you are an overgrown kid. Likewise, junior highers need encouragement just to be themselves and not try to be little adults. Your role should be that of an adult friend who sincerely likes them, cares about them, and tries to understand and help whenever possible.

Liking junior highers is not always something that comes naturally, especially as you grow older. Still, most of the time building a relationship with them is easier than you might think. It does require a commitment, as most relationships do, and it also requires cultivation and care to help it along. In other words, it's no different from any other kind of relationship—you have to work at it.

And don't just go through the motions. Sincerity is important in working with junior highers. They don't appreciate a person who is overrelating to them or who takes the approach that "I'm not really an adult, I'm one of you." What is most effective is consistency and genuineness. It doesn't make that much difference what you are or what you do, as long as you are not putting on a show. Sincerity is the key.

LEARNING TO HAVE PATIENCE

Junior-high workers definitely need to have patience. In many ways, patience is just like faith. It's "being sure of what we hope for and certain of what we do not see" (Heb. 11:1). The dictionary defines patience as "endurance, fortitude, or persistent courage in trying circumstances." There is no question that junior-high workers need *that* kind of patience. Why? Because, in junior-high ministry, "success" and "results" are almost nonexistent, at least in the ways most people understand 'those two words.

Ralph Waldo Emerson once wrote this about success: "I look on that man as happy who, when there is a question of success, looks into his work for a reply." He was correct, of course. People are going to be most happy when they examine their work and find that they have accomplished something significant and worthwhile.

But if your work is junior-high ministry, you may look into it and not find anything at all that looks or sounds like success. The only reply you may get is silence.

Most people who have worked with junior highers for any length of time will tell you that in junior-high ministry, you don't see too many "results." You learn to develop an "eternal perspective," which is another way of saying, "You'll get your reward in heaven."

For example, junior-high workers receive little in the way of affirmation and praise for what they do. Everyone, especially a volunteer, needs to be stroked a little bit, but in junior-high ministry, strokes are most often in short supply.

Little children are an ideal group to work with because they are so easy to please. Do something nice for them, and they'll make you feel like a hero.

Working with older youth and adults is also great for the ego. Even if you do poorly, at least a few will go out of their way to write thank-you notes, shake your hand, and offer words of encouragement.

But with junior highers, it's a different story. It's not uncommon to knock yourself out for this age group and rather than getting stroked, you get discipline problems. Instead of applause, you get sneers and snores. Unless you are prepared for it, this kind of affirmation can be very frustrating.

It's helpful to know that junior highers actually have a higher regard for the adults who work with them than any other age group, even though they have funny ways of expressing it. It usually takes a few years before they fully realize just how significant those adults are (or were). I will discuss this more fully a little later.

Another reason for patience is that junior-high workers rarely see the results or end product—what I call *visible impact*—of their work. Most people in the ministry want to think that their efforts actually make a difference in other people's lives. They would like for their ministry to "bear fruit" and produce tangible, visible results. It is encouraging for a pastor or teacher to know that his or her words are being taken to heart and being put into practice. It is gratifying for a counselor to know that an individual took his or her words of advice seriously and is now benefiting from them. Without a certain amount of visible impact, it would be difficult to continue.

But it is safe to say that such visible impact does not exist in junior-high ministry. You can get kids to repeat all the right words, to make all kinds of "decisions," and to behave themselves for varying periods of time. But real, lasting results will not be very evident while the kids are still junior highers.

A friend of mine recently took his junior-high group on a mission trip to Mexico. The trip was one part of a six-week discipleship course that he was conducting for his junior highers about Christian values. By allowing the group to see for themselves the poverty and the suffering of the poor people of Mexico, he hoped that his junior highers would be able to make better decisions about their values and priorities. Two weeks later after a fund-raising activity, my friend asked the group to make a choice: They could use the money they had raised to help feed and clothe the poor people they had visited in Mexico, or they could use it for a trip to an amusement park. The decision was theirs.

The group voted unanimously to go to the amusement park.

When something like this happens, it makes you wonder whether your "work" is making any difference at all. Normally, you hope that you see results reflected in some kind of positive behavior, but with junior highers, you just can't count on it. And it rarely has anything to do with how well or how poorly you are doing your job. Learning and growth in junior highers will be taking place even when their behavior seems to indicate otherwise.

Again, the best way to see the visible impact of junior-high ministry is to wait for a few years. Working with junior highers is a classic "sowing" ministry. Someone else will undoubtedly do the reaping.

I like to tell junior-high workers that their ministry is a lot like the ministry that Jesus had while he was on earth. Jesus spent three years with his disciples, yet he never saw any results while he was with them. Most of the disciples deserted Jesus when he needed them the most. He went to the cross without seeing his ministry come to fruition. It was not until later that the ministry of Jesus began to have visible impact. So it is when you work with junior highers.

LEARNING TO BE A GOOD LISTENER

Junior highers are at a point in their lives when they need someone who will listen to them. The old saying "children should be seen and not heard" doesn't go over very well with early adolescents. They want to be heard. They want to be taken seriously, and of course, the best way to take them seriously is to listen to what they have to say.

Listening has rightly been called "the language of love," and in junior-high ministry, it is also the key to a young person's heart. Adolescent psychologist Dr. Stephen Glenn, in his excellent series "Developing Capable Young People," has said that "when you take a young adolescent seriously, you are given a great deal of power and authority over him."[4] Be careful—don't interpret that to mean that the purpose of listening is to control or dominate junior highers. What it means is that when a junior higher is taken seriously by an adult, then that young person gives back to the adult *the right* to exercise power and authority over him. Said another way, if you listen to junior highers, they will listen to you. Junior-high workers who want to have a significant impact on the lives of young people would be well advised to develop their listening skills, rather than only their verbal skills.

A POSITIVE ATTITUDE AND
A SENSE OF HUMOR

Junior highers need to be around people who demonstrate a positive attitude, who smile a lot, and who know how to have fun. You can't be a "grouch" and be a very effective junior-high worker. You need to have a warm sense of humor.

This doesn't mean that you have to be a comedian. You don't have to be the stereotypical junior-high worker whose biggest asset is the ability to tell jokes and take a pie in the face. Junior-high ministry is more than fun and games. It does mean that you are mature enough not to take yourself, your junior highers, or your programs too seriously. You just need to be able to "loosen up" a bit.

I have met many junior-high workers who see themselves primarily as disciplinarians. Their job is to maintain law and order. The problem with that attitude is that many (if not most) discipline problems in junior-high ministry are self-inflicted by junior-high workers who are essentially negative and humorless. Those who approach junior-high ministry with an "army sergeant" mentality won't last very long. There are times when it is much better to try to see the humor in some of the outlandish or disruptive things that junior highers do, rather than to try to stop them with reprimands and threats of punishment.

When I first began running junior-high camps and retreats, I learned very quickly that the campers enjoyed most those activities that were clearly against the rules, such as conducting midnight raids on each others' cabins, having water balloon wars, and setting booby traps around their cabins. Rather than cracking down and punishing those who participated in such activities, we legalized virtually all of it. We had giant water balloon fights, we allowed secret raids each evening on unsuspecting cabins, and we even gave an award each day for the most inventive booby trap set by a cabin group. The results were quite positive, and the kids had a great camping experience.

There are some people who have a tendency to see the proverbial sugar bowl as being "half empty" and those who see it as being "half full." I prefer to see junior-high youth workers come from the second group—people who are able to look beyond the faults and inconsistencies of early adolescents to see the "big picture." Junior highers need someone who will laugh with them at their mistakes and who will let them know that they are loved even when they mess up.

GIVING THEM ENOUGH OF YOUR TIME

You may have sensed by now that good junior-high ministry could require a sizeable portion of your time. It does take time, after all, to build relationships and to pay attention to a group of young people, not to mention all the meetings, classes, outings, and the like. Time is a very important factor in the potential effectiveness of a junior-high worker in the church, and the time demands can be discouraging. Rarely does anyone have more than enough time to give to an activity. The problem is usually finding any time at all with today's busy schedules.

Speaking from personal experience, this shortage of time can be the downfall of any well-intentioned junior-high worker. You may like junior highers and have a strong desire to minister to them, but just be too busy to put that desire into practice. For this reason, I always list as a prerequisite for the junior-high worker a willingness to allocate enough of his or her time to do an adequate job. The actual amount of time will vary a great deal from person to person, but it is certain that it will take more than an hour or two on Sunday.

Time plays such an important role because it is tied up with the fact that junior highers view things pretty much in black and white categories. That is, you are either a friend to them or you are not. When you say one thing and fail (or are unable) to back it up with your actions, you run the risk of being categorized as a hypocrite. That, of course, is not always accurate, but proving otherwise can sometimes be difficult. Junior highers characteristically fail to understand adult obligations, and they often take this to mean that some task is more important than they are.

The bottom line here is that junior-high ministry must be more than good intentions. It does require time. When I look for someone to help with a junior-high group, I try to find someone who is not already committed to dozens of other jobs in the church, since I don't want these other jobs to rob them of the time they are going to need to build relationships with junior-high kids.

On the other hand, I have learned that a little bit of time is always better than no time at all. If you are a volunteer, as most junior-high workers are, you may have only one or two hours a week to do junior-high ministry. You may have time to call or visit only two kids all month. But that's great! Chances are that's more time than anyone else was able to give to those two kids all month, and God will bless that. Jesus fed a multitude with two fish; he can also work wonders with two hours.

The danger is overextending yourself. You have so much to do, and so little time in which to do it, that nothing gets done. If that sounds familiar, then perhaps you need to (1) make sure your responsibilities match up with the time you have available and (2) find others who can help share the load.

GETTING HELP WHEN IT'S NEEDED

You may be the kind of person who can do everything yourself, but it is more likely that if you are single-handedly ministering to the junior highers in your church, regardless of the size of the group, you could benefit from some help. Junior-high ministry is always best when it is a "team" ministry. If you are a youth director or Christian education director responsible for a number of age groups, you are also no doubt in need of other adults who can serve as junior-high sponsors or leaders.

How many? Usually the size of the group will dictate the exact number that is required. A good ratio is approximately one adult for every eight junior highers, although every group should have at least two adult leaders—one male and one female. The 1:8 ratio, although arbitrary, is based on the idea that it is difficult to establish relationships with many more than eight. It can be done, of course, but it's much more difficult, especially with the many other responsibilities of adult life. If you hope to be able to give some quality time to each person, it is wise not to bite off more than you can chew.

Another important consideration is the male-female balance of the group. If you are a male but your group is made up of quite a few girls, you should have a female co-worker who can relate to those girls as only another female can. Junior-high girls are just beginning to deal with their emerging womanhood, and they need adult women whom they can trust and confide in. The same is true for boys. It's not being sexist to recognize that boys should have men they can relate and look up to and girls should have women. Early adolescence is an important time of gender identification, and it helps to have good adult role models available.

A related problem for many young male junior-high workers is how to handle junior-high girls who "fall in love" with them. This also happens, although less frequently, with female junior-high workers and junior-high boys. I don't have an easy answer for that one, but one good way to prevent or rectify situations like this is (if you are male) to work with a woman who can help to minister to the girls in the group.

The problem, of course, is not usually the failure to know when more help is needed. The problem is knowing *whom* to enlist. For reasons already stated, there is rarely a waiting list of people who want to work with junior-high kids. Usually those who do emerge are what I call "chronic volunteerers"—people who have also volunteered for every other job in the church. They're usually fine folks, but they're volunteering for youth work for the wrong reasons. To wait for volunteers is usually not the best way to get the best people. The best way is to take the initiative yourself and seek out people who you have reason to believe would make capable junior-high workers.

Anyone who works as a teacher, counselor, youth-group sponsor, or in a similar capacity with junior highers in the church should be reasonably qualified to do so, that is, they should possess to some degree the qualifications previously described in this chapter. Again, no one has to be perfect. As a rule of thumb, I usually seek people who have the time and the willingness to give junior-high ministry a try and who seem like the kind of people who haven't repressed their own adolescence so much that they find it impossible to relate to or identify with junior highers. From that point, other necessary or helpful skills may be developed.

When looking for junior-high workers, I have found that it is generally best to rule out high-school students. They usually lack the maturity necessary to minister with much depth. When I worked as a junior-high camp director, I always had the most difficulty with groups that had high-school aged cabin counselors.

We commonly had to discipline male counselors who had become overly zealous about "counseling" some of the more mature female campers long after the evening meetings were over. High-school students may be fully capable of assisting in many areas of the junior-high program, but in most cases it is better to seek more mature leadership.

College students often make very good junior-high workers, but there are problems common to this age group as well. One is that they may be somewhat transient—here this semester, gone the next, or away for the summer. It is best to find people who can give the junior-high group a degree of stability over two or three years if possible.

One junior-high ministry that I am familiar with asks a three-year commitment from its sponsors. Each sponsor (a man, for example) at the beginning of this term is given a group of six to eight seventh-grade boys, and he works with those boys for three full years (through seventh, eighth, and ninth grade) until they move on to the high-school department of the church. Of course, in practice, this model is no more free from breakdown than any other, but the reasoning is sound. For three years, each junior higher in the group has someone who knows him well and really notices whenever he is having difficulty or is making progress. The end result of such a plan should be a lower dropout rate as well as a more effective ministry.

Parents often are willing to work with the junior-high group and, depending on who the parents are, that can be either good or bad. Some parents feel they need to spend as much time as they can with their own kids, so they want to work with the junior-high group. This is not all bad, but neither is it the best motivation for becoming involved in junior-high ministry. Some parents feel that because they have junior highers of their own, that automatically qualifies them as experts and therefore as good junior-high workers. Maybe so, maybe not. Others are concerned that the junior-high group is not quite up to par by their standards, and they want to help out, at least for as long as their kids are in it.

Parents can and should be involved in the junior-high program in some way, but there are some potential problems with parents doubling as junior-high workers. They may be overly protective of their own children or perhaps too close to them to deal with them in an objective manner. It's difficult to be neutral with your own kids. You can give objective, empathetic advice to other people's kids, but it's difficult to do that with your own.

A bigger problem is that kids are more than likely going to be intimidated by the presence of their parents in the youth group, which prevents them from opening up as they might under normal conditions. Most junior highers are involved, either quietly or overtly, in a struggle to free themselves from parental domination, and they usually need adults other than their parents to relate to during this time.

Having said that, however, I would not rule out parents of junior highers as leaders for the junior-high group, especially if they sincerely want to be involved and appear to be qualified to do so. It's strictly a judgment call. I would be very selective if I were in a position to decide and I would try to help such parents to avoid problems that might arise.

So to whom can you go for help? Whom does that leave?

Young adults, either single or married and in their twenties and thirties, make excellent junior-high workers. Young couples with no children or with young children often make a wonderful husband and wife team in the junior-high group. Older adults whose children have grown, or those of retirement age, are often well qualified and may be willing to work with the junior highers of the church. So long as they enjoy the kids and are able to understand and communicate with them, they have all that it takes. Many times kids will love and respect older folks more than those closer to their own age.

One of the most creative junior-high workers I have ever met is in his sixties. He teaches a Sunday school class of seventh grade boys in a small town in Oregon. Once a month he has his class wear old clothes to church and instead of attending services that week, they all climb into the back of his camper and go fishing. He provides the boys with bait, tackle, and even shows them how to tie flies. And according to him, he gets more teaching done along the banks of a stream once a month than he is able to accomplish during the three weeks spent in the classroom. I wouldn't doubt it at all.

OTHER PLACES TO GO FOR HELP

The important thing to keep in mind is that there are lots of ways to make your job a little easier as a junior-high worker. You don't have to do it all by yourself or start from scratch with everything. Get help when it's needed, either by recruiting additional junior-high workers to share the load or by making use of other people and resources. Just keep in mind that you will have to go after these things yourself. Help rarely comes calling on its own.

There is an abundance of printed resources that are loaded with ideas to make the programing end of junior-high ministry a lot less time-consuming. You don't have to be original with everything you do. I have always maintained that the essence of creativity is the ability to copy well what has already been done, and this holds true with youth work as well. Why reinvent the wheel? Many hundreds of hours have gone into developing the resources that are at your disposal, and the more you use other people's good ideas, the easier it becomes to create ideas of your own.

There are numerous seminars, workshops, and training events held at various times of the year all over the country, sponsored by many different denominations and by independent youth ministry organizations, like *Youth Specialties*. It is not always convenient to attend those events that require a great deal of travel, time, or expense, but these conferences are excellent ways to get a shot in the arm when you may be needing it most.

In addition, there are undoubtedly junior-high workers from other churches in your area who would probably appreciate getting together with you periodically for sharing ideas and support. At times you will find that you are able to pool resources with other churches and possibly schedule some activities together. This is especially beneficial for smaller youth groups.

You may also find it helpful to form a support group of parents and other interested persons in the church who are able to meet with you whenever necessary to discuss some of your concerns, to help with planning, and to pray for the junior-high ministry of the church. There are probably a number of people in your congregation who are unable to work with the junior highers week after week but who have much to offer in an advisory or supporting role.

The kids themselves can be a big help to you as well. You don't have to do everything for them. Junior highers are capable of taking on responsibility, and they usually enjoy it. It's a good rule of thumb, however, not to give them more than they can handle or complete within a reasonable length of time. They can become easily frustrated or bored with the whole thing if it seems too big. Junior highers are great starters and lousy finishers. But be on the lookout for ways they can be involved. Not only will the kids benefit, but they will also save you a lot of work in the process.

A final note on this subject: Remember that your greatest resource is God. Junior-high ministry is a calling from God, and he will provide you with the strength and the resources to pull it off. If you feel inadequate, great! God will be able to use you much more than the one who thinks he needs nothing more than all of his incredible talents, abilities, and resources. Be yourself and let God do the rest.

Bathe your junior-high ministry in prayer. Pray for each of your young people specifically and your program and activities generally. Depend upon God to take whatever you are able to do and to bless and multiply it. He will!

Part II

FROM CHILDREN
TO ADULTS

3.
THE CHANGEABLE
WORLD OF EARLY
ADOLESCENCE

The next few chapters will deal with the important characteristics of junior highers. There are certain characteristics that make junior highers different from other people, and we'll treat them in five areas: the physical, social, intellectual, emotional, and spiritual. While it is convenient to discuss each of these areas individually, it is important to keep in mind that these categories are very artificial. Life really isn't divided up that way. But in the interest of clarity, it helps to take each of these areas one by one. As we look at these areas and discuss the characteristics of junior highers, we will also deal with their implications. Our aim will be to relate what is known about junior highers to ministering to them in the church. It is not enough to merely describe junior-high kids. Most people know what one looks and acts like. What we want to do is see how all of these characteristics affect the way we work with and relate to junior highers.

THE NEEDS OF EARLY ADOLESCENCE
It always makes good sense to start with needs when you are attempting to minister to a particular group of people. Need-centered ministry is simply discovering or defining a person's specific needs, and then trying, if possible, to find effective ways to meet those needs. To use a comparison, a doctor will diagnose a patient carefully before treating that person or before prescribing a cure. Obviously, not every patient requires the same kind of treatment. What is good for one may be disastrous for another. Just

49

because something worked for one patient doesn't mean it will be helpful for all. The doctor must begin with each patient's specific needs.

I heard a story once about a young boy who got an archery set for his birthday. A few days later, the boy ran into the house and excitedly asked his father to come look where he had been shooting arrows into the side of an old barn. His father went outside and was amazed by what he saw. There on the side of the barn were several targets, and dead center in the bull's-eye of each target was one of the boy's arrows. The father was naturally impressed and very proud of his young Robin Hood. He asked the boy how he had learned so fast to shoot so straight. The boy replied, "Easy. I just shot the arrows first, and then drew the targets around each one."

It is unfortunate that a similar approach is often used in the church. Programs are a lot like arrows; people are like targets. The tendency is often to "draw" people around programs, rather than to create programs that are truly "on target," meeting needs. This is no doubt encouraged by all the "It worked for me and it will work for you" books and seminars that offer the very latest in techniques, ideas, strategies, and the like. Program ideas are very important and helpful, of course (some of my favorites are included in this book), but that's not the place to start. Every idea or method should be carefully chosen on the basis of whether or not it meets the particular needs of the individuals in the group. There are many ideas that work, but not all of them meet needs.

This brings us back to the characteristics of junior-high kids. This is our target group. Early adolescents offer us a variety of needs that have to be dealt with if effective ministry is to take place. Junior highers differ significantly from other age groups. A good junior-high worker should know what those differences are and then act or program accordingly, in the best interests of the kids.

Unfortunately, there remains a considerable gap between what we know about junior highers and how we treat them. This is true not only in our churches but in the public schools as well. According to Don Wells, principal of the Carolina Friends School:

> When attempting to construct a program for the early adolescent, one is immediately struck by the wide disparity between the data we have on the early adolescent and the programmatic response we devise . . .

1) *Fact:* Early adolescents need to try on a wide variety of roles. *Response:* We class them in . . . a few roles to make them a manageable lot.

2) *Fact:* Early adolescents vary enormously . . . in physical, mental and emotional maturity and capability. *Response:* In schools, chronological age is still the overwhelming factor used in grouping students.

3) *Fact:* During early adolescence the development of control over one's life through conscious decision making is crucial. *Response:* Adults make all meaningful decisions for almost all early adolescents almost all of the time, but do give the early adolescent the "freedom" to make "safe" decisions.

4) *Fact:* Early adolescence is an age where all natural forces (muscular, intellectual, glandular, emotional) are causing precipitous peaks and troughs in their entire being. *Response:* We demand internal consistency of the early adolescent, and in schools even punish some for not achieving this consistent state despite the fact that it is totally impossible for many to achieve at this point in development.

5) *Fact:* Early adolescents need space and experience to "be" different persons at different times. *Response:* We expect them to "be" what they said they were last week because otherwise we cannot use forethought in dealing with them.

6) *Fact:* Early adolescents are preoccupied by physical and sexual concerns, frightened by their perceived inadequacy. *Response:* We operate with them each day not as though this were a minor matter in their lives, but as though such concerns did not exist at all.

7) *Fact:* Early adolescents need a distinct feeling of present importance, a present relevancy of their own lives now. *Response:* We place them in institutions called "junior-high schools," which out of hand stress their subordinate status to their next maturational stage, and then feed them a diet of watered down "real stuff."[1]

In the next five chapters, we will focus on many of the characteristics of early adolescents that have relevance for junior-high workers in the church and that demand our attention. Keep in mind that I do not intend to duplicate or replace any of the outstanding writing on early adolescence by leading doctors, psychologists, educators, and researchers. All of these people are more qualified than I to give the subject a more scholarly and thorough treatment. In fact, I cannot overemphasize to you the importance of reading as much as you can about this age group from other sources, particularly the work of Erik Erikson, David Elkind, Joan Lipsitz, Peter Blos, J.M. Tanner, Jean Piaget, and Lawrence Kohlberg. Although we will only be scratching the surface, we will try to cover, in as much depth as necessary, those areas of special significance to the junior-high worker in the church.

THE VARIABILITY OF EARLY ADOLESCENCE

Throughout this book, I will be making quite a few generalizations, which is a very dangerous thing to do when you are talking about people. It's especially hazardous when talking about junior highers, since no two junior highers are alike. In fact, the preceding sentence is about the only generalization that can be made about junior highers with any real accuracy.

The word that best describes this age group is the word *variability*. That is to say, they vary tremendously from one person to the next. To know that a young person is thirteen is to know virtually nothing important about that person, except perhaps his grade in school.[2] Most thirteen-year-olds are in the eighth grade. Other than that, there isn't much you can say about that young person with any accuracy. He or she could be a fast developer, a slow developer, or somewhere in between.

Joan Lipsitz has noted that "it is not unusual to find a six-year difference in biological age between slowly developing boys and rapidly developing girls in the same classroom."[3] This observation is based on the fact that it is "normal" for there to be a four-year spread in the average age of the onset of puberty. Add to that the fact that it is "normal" for girls to be about two years ahead of boys. This means that there could be a six-year difference between a late-blooming thirteen-year-old boy and an early-developing thirteen-year-old girl.

Most of us who have worked with junior highers for any length of time have seen this phenomenon firsthand. There in your "eighth grade" Sunday school class is a girl who looks old enough to be dating college guys (and she probably is). And sitting right behind her is a freckle-faced boy who looks about nine years old and who talks with a high-pitched voice. Which one is the real eighth grader? Which of these young people do you create your eighth-grade curriculum for? These are questions that will continue to plague those who work with this age group, and unfortunately there are no simple answers. "And here we are considering only biological age," adds Lipsitz. "There is such extreme variability among individuals who are changing not only physically, but also socially, emotionally, and intellectually, that the label of chronological age . . . may be the most misleading social organizer that we have adopted."[4]

This is one of the reasons it is important that you do not look at your junior-high group as a "group." Instead, you must see them as Jason, Michelle, Christin, Mike, Nate, Dylan, Abbie, and Megan. Your group is a collection of persons who are all at different places in their development and who have different needs at different times. We will be saying a lot more in this book about the importance of relationships, but as you can see, the need for a personal, one-on-one kind of ministry becomes obvious when you consider the variability of this age group.

We may need to find better ways to group junior highers than by age or by grade in school. Some junior-high ministries have experimented with grouping kids according to maturity level. Others have tried grouping kids according to interest, using a variety of electives and other activities from which kids could choose. It is doubtful that there exists a simple, clear-cut method that takes the variability of this age group into consideration and works for everyone. One thing is clear: The junior-high worker who is concerned about individual kids will do a better job meeting their needs than the one who is more concerned about groups.

Nevertheless, there are some things that can be said about junior-high kids in general, and I won't hesitate in this book to say them. While we cannot say that all kids are the same, we can say that the majority of young people between the ages of eleven and fourteen do have many developmental tasks and characteristics in common. But don't try to put the kids you work with in a box. Some kids will be way ahead of schedule, others far behind, and some kids will skip certain stages altogether.

4.
PHYSICAL DEVELOPMENT IN EARLY ADOLESCENTS

PUBERTY STRIKES!

> Puberty, next to birth itself, is the most drastic change we experience in life, but unlike birth, we are acutely aware of the exciting transitions through which we pass.[1]

Probably the most important thing we can say about physical development in junior highers is that they are going through puberty. Their bodies are going through an enormous change. It only happens once in a person's lifetime; the child is transformed into an adult. Physically, both boys and girls develop into men and women mostly while they are in junior-high school.

In the United States, the average age for menarche, when a girl has her first menstrual period, is 12.9 years. The female adolescent growth spurt actually begins much earlier around 9.6 years. Its peak velocity is about age 11.8. Comparable milestones occur almost two years later for boys.[2] This is why girls are usually bigger than boys during early adolescence and are more fully developed. The boys don't catch up with the girls physically until around age fifteen. (See chart on next page.) This, of course, creates some problems in communication and relationships between the boys and the girls. The boys are starting to take an interest in the girls (finally), but to their chagrin, most of the girls are more interested in older boys!

While the above figures are fairly accurate, they are not absolute. As I noted earlier, it is not unusual for two boys who are the same age to be as much as four years apart in physical development during early adolescence.

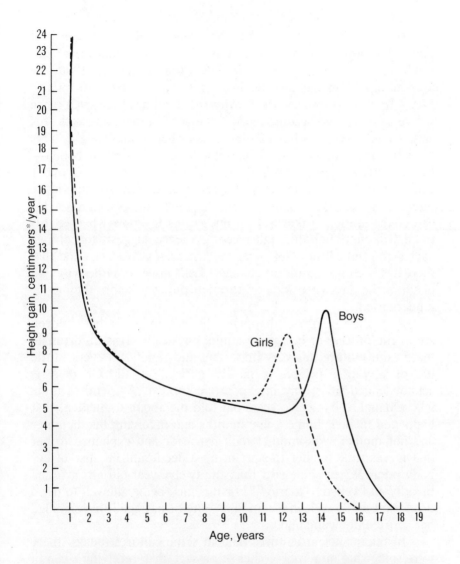

Typical velocity curves for length or height in boys and girls. These curves represent the velocity of the typical boy or girl at a given instant. From J. M. Tanner, R. H. Whitehouse, and M. Takaishi, "Standards from Birth to Maturity for Height, Weight Height Velocity and Weight Velocity; British Children, 1965," *Archives of Disease in Childhood* 41 (1966); 455-71. (*A centimeter equals .39 inch.)

Most people are aware that the average age for the onset of puberty is lower today than it was, say, a hundred years ago. Studies in the United States have shown that in the year 1900, the average age of menarche was 14.2 years, compared with today's 12.9.[3] In other countries, the downward trend has been even more severe as they have become more "civilized." Coinciding with this earlier maturation has been an increase in height and weight. This has led many experts to think that modern society's eating habits— better nutrition, more protein and calories—have been a major contributor to earlier puberty. Bigger people seem to experience puberty earlier. But no one seems to know the exact reason for earlier maturation. Likewise, no one seems to know whether this trend will continue, although recent evidence suggests that things have stabilized considerably over the last twenty-five years and that there has been no significant change.[4] Let's hope so. Otherwise, we may see the day when kids go through puberty before they enter kindergarten.

Regardless of when it happens, the bottom line is that children are in the process of becoming adults physically. It is unfortunate that in our culture this very important and significant event in the life of a young person is hardly noticed at all. Or if it is acknowledged, it is only in a negative context. A friend of mine whose daughter is twelve years old told me about an incident that happened in their home a few months ago involving his daughter and her mother. The mother took her aside and explained to her that it was time for her to start using a deodorant because of her body odor. When she heard this, the twelve-year-old girl grinned broadly and yelled "Hooray!" For this girl, being allowed to use a deodorant was a welcome symbolic "rite of passage" that signaled her entry into womanhood.

In many ancient cultures (and in some cultures today), there were somewhat more noble rites of passage than receiving a can of deodorant. For example, as soon as a boy or girl manifested the physical signs of adulthood (menarche, pubic hair, and so on), there would be ceremonial rites of passage to make one's passing from childhood into adulthood a matter of public record. For girls, these rites often included such events as the celebration of the arrival of the first menstruation, formal training in sexual matters, and instruction in cooking, clothes making, and the like.

Boys, who do not experience such a well-defined and observable event as menarche, would sometimes be taken off in the company of the men, perhaps circumcised, tutored in the duties and privileges of manhood, and allowed to emerge "officially" as a man. Among some American Indian tribes, a boy would go out alone on a "vision quest." He would then return, reborn, with a new name, his name as a man.[5]

Today, this passage from childhood to adulthood is not nearly so clear-cut or brief. We ask our junior highers, who are emerging adults, to wait another six or seven years before claiming their adulthood. No doubt here's the reason for many of the problems and frustrations faced by modern teenagers, particularly sexual problems. They have adult bodies, but they must keep them on hold. They are required to muzzle their natural urges, which for some is a very difficult thing to do.

It is interesting to note that the trend toward an earlier onset of puberty in recent times, combined with modern culture's trend toward later marriages, more education, and the like, has created a special group of people that many cultures never had to deal with before—teenagers. In fact, the term "teenager" was not really a part of the English language until the 1940s, and it was not until then (or later) that "youth work" began to be perceived as necessary. Until recently, there were few books, resources, or organizations specializing in youth ministry because youth work was still in its infancy. Junior-high ministry is *still* in its infancy. Welcome to the frontier!

What's Happening?

The junior higher's body changes in many ways during puberty, and these changes are accompanied by an equal number of puzzling new experiences—some exciting, some embarrassing, and others just plain awful. When these "perils of puberty" occur, it's hard for many early adolescents to understand them or adjust to them. What makes it even worse is that no one talks much about them either, and those who do are often misinformed.

PHYSICAL CHANGES DURING ADOLESCENCE

MALES	FEMALES
Development of penis and testicles	Development of ovaries and uterus
Pubic hair growth	Pubic hair growth
Involuntary ejaculation	Onset of menstruation
Enlargement of neck	Breast development
Broadening of shoulders	Widening of hips
Growth of armpit hair	Growth of armpit hair
Marked growth of hair on face and body	Slight growth of hair on face and body
Deepening of voice	Slight deepening of voice
Increase in activity of sweat glands	Increase in activity of sweat glands
Growth spurt in height and weight	Growth spurt in height and weight
Growth of muscle tissue	Growth of fat-bearing cells

For girls, one of the most noticeable of these changes is a general acceleration in both height and weight, a widening of the hips, and the appearance of breasts. At this age, girls become softer, rounder, and grow very concerned about their "figures." They want to look good in a bathing suit, and they want boys to notice them.

This can be a very frustrating time for girls who are concerned that they are growing too much or too little in the wrong places and who insist upon comparing themselves with others or the girls they see in the fashion magazines. Breasts, especially, have become such a preoccupation in our society, that it is not surprising that girls with small breasts often fear that boys will never like them. Girls worry, too, if one breast grows faster than the other, which is not unusual. Dr. Maryanne Collins, pediatrician and specialist in adolescent medicine, has pointed this out: "When a young girl starts to develop breasts, one side always enlarges first. Invariably mothers and daughters get concerned because they do not realize that this is normal."[6] Girls also worry if their breasts enlarge too quickly. A girl with "too much" is often the object of considerable ridicule from other girls and some rather unpleasant joking from the boys. Most girls could benefit from some assurance at this point that beauty and sex appeal is rarely dependent on the breasts or any other part of the anatomy for that matter. Breasts, like women, come in all shapes and sizes.

Junior-high girls also usually experience their first period, which can be a real shock if they aren't prepared for it. Accidents occur at the worst times and are very embarrassing. Menstruation for junior-high girls is just like it is for older women, so it is frequently accompanied by abdominal pains, lack of energy, and occasional irritability. Also, it takes a while before most girls have their period on a regular twenty-eight day cycle. They might go three months without having a period and then have two very close together. This can cause a lot of worry, as well. Hopefully, someone is able to assure them that all this is normal.

For boys, their first frustration with puberty is that they don't develop as early as the girls do. But when they do experience the onset of puberty, they grow rapidly and unevenly. It is not uncommon for boys to grow as much as six inches in one year, yet the arms, legs, and trunk may grow disproportionately and result in awkwardness and clumsiness. Just when a boy is becoming more coordinated, puberty strikes and his forward progress may be set back. Some boys worry because they aren't growing very rapidly and think they are too short. Appetites increase dramatically at this age, as well. Most junior-high boys can easily outeat adults. Another noticeable change is the deepening of the voice, which creates embarrassing moments when it decides to change right in the middle of a sentence. Acne (pimples on the face) is another peril of puberty that is common to both boys and girls.

Perhaps the most telltale sign of approaching manhood is the emergence of pubic hair. For boys, pubic hair is similar in significance to breasts for girls. Until you grow a crop of pubic hair around the genitals, your manhood remains in doubt. Taking a shower after a P.E. class can be a traumatic experience for a slow developer. I have visited boys' locker rooms at junior-high schools where no one took showers at all. When I was running junior-high camps, it was not uncommon for boys hoping to avoid embarrassment to go all week without changing their underwear.

The event for boys that parallels menarche for girls is the first ejaculation. Usually this occurs while the boy is asleep, hence the term "wet dream." Unprepared for this, some boys think they just wet the bed—more worry and guilt. Other worries include the size of one's penis (in comparison with others that they have seen or heard about) and spontaneous erections (occurring at the most inappropriate times). Masturbation is also common with this age group.

A friend of mine recently related to me an incident that illustrates the "fence-walking" that young adolescents sometimes do between childhood and adulthood during puberty. My friend took a group of junior highers to summer camp, and after arrival, he noticed that one of the kids had left his suitcase on the bus. Unable to find the camper to whom it belonged, he opened up the suitcase to see if there might be a name or some other clue to the camper's identity. Inside the suitcase, among the clothing and other personal articles, he found two very interesting items: a can of Play-Doh and a copy of *Penthouse* magazine. The suitcase belonged to a twelve-year-old boy.

Early adolescents are experiencing some extraordinary physical changes during the junior-high years, and while they are aware of them, they often do not anticipate or understand them. If we really believe in need-centered ministry, then it would seem only natural to consider a junior higher's need to know about the changes taking place in his or her body and the need to be assured that what is happening is good, not bad. God is not trying to make life miserable for them. They need to know that these changes are normal, not something to be ashamed of nor afraid of. Puberty happened to all of us, and we came though it pretty well. So will they.

A New Awareness of the Body

With the onset of puberty comes a newly acquired awareness of the body. Junior highers become very concerned with their appearance—whether or not they are good looking or attractive and whether or not they measure up to others their own age. They are, in their own secret fears, growing too rapidly, too slowly, too unevenly, too tall, or developing too much in all the wrong places. And for many, these fears are justified. Physical growth can be very uneven and unpredictable during early adolescence, which can be the source of much anxiety and grief. Recent studies have shown that worry "about my looks" peaks at the eighth grade: 69 percent of girls and 49 percent of boys in that grade list this as their main worry.[7] Here is how one teenager described what was happening to her:

> Every day, just about, something new seems to be happening to this body of mine and I get scared sometimes. I'll wake up in the middle of the night and I can't go back to sleep, and I toss and I turn and I can't stop my mind; it's racing fast, and everything is coming into it, and I think of my two best friends, and how their faces are all broken out, and I worry mine will break out, too, but so far it hasn't, and I think of my sizes, and I can't get it out of my head—the chest size and the stomach size and what I'll be wearing and whether I'll be able to fit into this kind of dress or the latest swimsuit. Well, it goes on and on, and I'm dizzy, even though it's maybe one o'clock in the morning, and there I am, in bed, so how can you be dizzy?

> Everything is growing and changing. I can see my mother watching me. I can see everyone watching me. There are times I think I see people watching me when they really couldn't care less! My dad makes a point of not staring, but he catches his look, I guess. I'm going to be "big-chested"; that's how my mother describes herself! I have to figure out how to dress so I feel better—I mean, so I don't feel strange, with my bosom just sticking out at everyone! I have to decide if I should shave my legs! I will! Damn! I wish a lot of the time I could just go back to being a little girl, without all these problems and these decisions![8]

She describes quite vividly in those two paragraphs how many junior highers feel. They worry tremendously about their appearance, and about how their bodies will turn out when they stop growing. Ordinarily, it's not a neurotic kind of worrying. Most kids don't lose sleep over their pimples, although some do. Although there are actual cases on record of young people who have committed suicide (or attempted it) because they perceived themselves as being ugly, such cases are extreme. Usually this worry is a hidden fear that affects the lives of young people in ways they are not even aware of at the time. For example, the slow developer who feels inadequate or out of place may try to compensate by becoming withdrawn or boisterous. Most junior highers require much more privacy than ever before. They will lock themselves in the bathroom for long periods of time while they examine themselves or try to improve their appearance.

Privacy is very important for early adolescents. At junior-high camps, it is not uncommon for kids to hang towels and blankets all around the bunk beds in their cabins to have private places to change clothes during the week. This is normal and to be expected because they don't want people to see them with their clothes off. I visited a junior high recently and I noticed that in the bathrooms the doors were missing from all the toilet stalls. I found out later that the school authorities had removed the doors because kids were smoking cigarettes inside the stalls. They believed that removing the doors would prevent such behavior. Unfortunately, what it prevented was not smoking, but using the toilet. They wound up with an entire school full of constipated kids.

Undoubtedly the biggest reason that junior highers are obsessed with their appearance and their physical development is that it dramatically affects their social lives. When my children were younger, they could make instant friends with anyone their own age. At the park, for instance, they would play with any other children who were there, regardless of race, creed, color, looks, or sex. But as children grow older and get closer to the onset of puberty, this innocence fades. Kids become much more selective in their associations. Suddenly there emerges a "popular" group and an "unpopular" group. Popular kids don't have much to do with unpopular kids, and vice versa. It's an extremely rigid caste system that lasts for years, and it is particularly noticeable during the junior-high years. To be unpopular is terrible in the eyes of most kids, and of course, it's everyone's dream to be counted among the elite. When we are in this select group, acceptance by others, positions of leadership, and life "happily ever after" are virtually assured.

What is it that makes a person popular or unpopular? Most of the time it will have something to do with physical characteristics, such as how you look or how well developed you are. Early developing boys who are athletic, tall, and good looking tend to be the most popular. Girls who are pretty, have attractive figures, nice hair, and so on are likely to be popular. If you are ugly (or just plain), short, fat, or "flat," you are doomed. Unfortunately, this is made even worse by modern culture's overemphasis on being beautiful and sexy (as seen on TV and in magazines). For this reason, junior highers place a great deal of emphasis on physical characteristics. For them, it's a matter of social survival.

In Judy Blume's book *Letters to Judy*, there are a number of revealing letters that the author has received from young people who are very unhappy with their bodies. The following letter from a twelve-year-old girl is typical:

> Dear Judy,
>
> Hi, my name is Emily. I am twelve years old and live in Kansas. In fifth grade I had a lot of boyfriends, but now I am in seventh grade and I have none. It is because I am *flat*. All the boys tease me and call me "Board." Sometimes I feel like crying. All my friends talk about their periods and about shaving. I am afraid to ask my mother for a razor or a bra or a deodorant. One day I took my brother's deodorant so I would have some for gym. . . .[9]

A junior-high girl may become preoccupied with her appearance because she may have the idea that her entire future is dependent on it. She may think that if she isn't attractive, she may face not only being unpopular, but also she won't have dates, she won't get married, she won't be able to get a job or have children and so on. This view of the future, distorted as it may be, leaves some girls in a state of depression and despair. Others will embark on a strenuous program to repair whatever "defects" they may have with cosmetics, exercises, diets, and an endless quest for that miracle product that will make them look like Miss Cover Girl. And tragically, there are some young adolescent girls who develop serious eating disorders (anorexia and bulimia) because they are afraid of gaining weight.

In the surveys I have taken with junior highers, nearly all list as their heroes the most glamorous people in show business or in

63

sports. Their favorite television programs are those featuring heroic, beautiful, sexy, almost superhuman characters who are always successful and, more importantly, well liked and admired by everyone. Every junior higher fantasizes about being such a person. In response to the question "If you could change anything about yourself, what would it be?" young people invariably list physical improvements—a new nose, new hair, new face, new shape, or a whole new body.

This dissatisfaction with themselves unfortunately causes some young people to have a deep resentment toward God who gets blamed for their lack of physical perfection. I heard one junior higher tell another, "When God was passing out noses, you thought he said roses, and asked for a big red one!"

On the other hand, the message of the gospel can be quite appealing to junior highers at this very point. They may feel inadequate or inferior because of their failure to measure up to the world's criteria for beauty or success, but Christ offers hope in the midst of all that. No one is plain or ordinary in the sight of God. We are all created in his image, which makes each of us a reflection of the beauty of God. We are special, despite the world's standards, because God loves us.

A youth-worker friend of mine used a very creative object lesson to illustrate to his junior highers that "beauty is only skin deep." He wrapped up some garbage in gift-wrapping paper and tied a nice ribbon around it. He also put a nice gift in a plain paper sack. Then he played a game with the junior highers and told the winner of the game to choose either package as a prize—the pretty one or the paper sack. Naturally the beautifully-wrapped package, containing the garbage, was chosen. The point was not missed by the kids: What is on the outside doesn't always reveal what is on the inside. We sometimes look only at the "outward appearance," but God looks into the heart. As Christians, we need to try to see things God's way and look for the "inner beauty" in each other. (By the way, the disappointed young person who chose the garbage was also awarded the paper sack containing the nice prize after the lesson was learned.)

We need to help kids understand the message of the gospel

concerning human worth, but we also need to take their feelings seriously. Even though they may be confident that God looks into their hearts, they are also confident that their friends look at their outward appearances, and that carries more weight at this particular time in their lives. Still, we need to model for them a different standard of behavior. We cannot let our actions contradict the very gospel that we teach. For example, we need to love the least attractive kids in our youth groups just as much as the most attractive ones. We must avoid using "put-downs" aimed at them or making fun of their physical shortcomings. Put-downs really hurt at this age. We need to treat each person with respect.

We should also be careful about parading in front of them glamorous Christian celebrities—former beauty queens, football heroes, and so on. We need to let kids know that God can use them, even though they may not be beautiful, athletic, or famous.

Avoid Embarrassing Them Needlessly

Junior highers can be very cruel at times and take every opportunity to point out deficiencies in each other whenever it is to their advantage. They think that by making fun of someone else, they are making themselves look superior. Usually junior highers are able to bounce back without any problem after some good-natured ribbing, but put-downs, ridicule, and the accompanying embarrassment can be very damaging to relationships and to self-esteem. It is important, therefore, that as much as possible we avoid situations in which kids might be looked down on because of ability, handicap, appearance, or physical development in general.

As a junior higher, I was a slow developer and not as athletic as other boys my age. Because of that, I did not enjoy P.E. classes at school. I enjoyed playing games and good competition as much as the other kids, but I hated to "choose up teams." I was inevitably chosen last, and it was humiliating every time it happened, even though I didn't blame anyone for not choosing me first. I was labeled a "klutz," but a few years later I caught up with most of my classmates in high school and did fairly well in athletic competition.

This is why I have included in this book some great games that almost anyone can play regardless of skill or ability. Why make junior highers suffer through games like football, basketball, and volleyball when only a few people can excel at them? There are plenty of other games available that are fun, physical, and very competitive (which junior highers love) but downplay athletic ability. These are the kind of games we should play with junior highers. I visited a junior high gym class recently and watched a seventh grade coed volleyball game. What a disaster! The kids hated it and couldn't wait for the period to be over because most of them were unable to return the ball successfully over the net. I was tempted to take over the class and show them a few games that were both fun and easy to play.

Despite all that you or anyone else can do, there is no good way to prevent junior highers from experiencing some embarrassment as long as they are around other people. It's normal and inevitable. But a good junior-high worker will at least be sensitive in this area, avoid put-downs and ridicule, and try to find ways to help each person to feel accepted, liked, and an important part of the group.

Help Them Find Affirmation in Other Areas

When I was in the ninth grade, I was arrested for shoplifting. My best friend and I were caught trying to walk out of a store with our coats lined with merchandise. That ended my brief career as a big-time crook. Like most adolescent shoplifters, my friend and I never needed anything we took. In fact, we usually gave most of it to our friends at school. It was just an exciting game, a challenge, and in retrospect, it was mostly a way for us to prove our manhood, both to ourselves and to others. We hadn't been able to prove it any other way. We had tried out for the freshman football and baseball teams and were unsuccessful. We weren't very popular. So we needed some way to show that we were courageous, adventurous tough guys, and for a while, shoplifting was how we did it. It made us look "big" in the eyes of our peers.

This kind of thinking is not uncommon with early adolescents who are slow developers or who have deep feelings of inferiority. The drive to be accepted by one's peers is strong and may cause junior highers to try to compensate for their lack of physical prowess in undesirable or self-destructive ways. Smoking, drinking, drug abuse, sexual promiscuity, rowdy behavior, vandalism, foul language, fighting, joining gangs, running away from home, and breaking the law are only some possible manifestations of this.

On the other hand, it is possible for kids to achieve the peer acceptance, ego satisfaction, and the like through positive and constructive means. After my life of crime in the ninth grade, I became interested in graphic art—drawing cartoons, designing posters, and painting signs. Soon this became my "thing." Everyone would come to me for art work, and gradually those feelings of inferiority diminished. I felt proud that the most popular kids in the school would ask me to help them with their publicity for school activities or for their student-body election campaigns.

Early adolescents need ways to gain a positive identity and a feeling of self-worth, and an important part of a junior-high worker's ministry can be to help kids find ways to accomplish this. Art, music, writing, program planning, public speaking, service, dramatics, leadership, teaching, sports, humor, or just helping out are all possibilities. Slow developers, especially, should be given opportunities whenever possible to affirm themselves in areas in which they can excel. Build on their assets and help them feel good about themselves even though they may not be winning the battle on the physical front.

SEX AND THE SINGLE JUNIOR HIGHER

With the onset of puberty comes the advent of sexual activity. This includes such things as increased attraction to the opposite sex, "crushes," "going steady," touching, petting—everything up to and including sexual intercourse. Many junior highers are sexually active. The 1984 Search Institute study "Young Adolescents and their Parents" (a survey of over 8,000 young adolescents from a variety of churches) revealed that 15 percent of 7th graders, 17 percent of 8th graders, and 20 percent of 9th graders answered yes to this question: "Have you ever had sexual intercourse ('gone all the way' or 'made love')?"[10] Other studies have revealed that the only age group for which the birth rate is not decreasing is that of fifteen-year-olds and under.[11]

While statistics like these may surprise us and make us aware that kids are becoming sexually active at a younger age, it is important to remember that today's young adolescents are not *that* different from adolescents of a generation or two ago. In 1954, William Carlos Williams wrote, "These kids get to be twelve or thirteen and they explode. They'll tell you that—energy is pushing through them, and some say they're going to ride with it, enjoy it, and not worry!"[12] Sexual feelings and desires during early adolescence are not new. It's a normal part of growing up. What is new is that today's young people are living in a very different world. In today's hedonistic culture, with its overemphasis on sex in movies, television, popular music, advertising, and just about everywhere else, kids are moving from A to Z much sooner than ever before.

Teaching Junior Highers about Sex

When I was in junior-high school, I automatically assumed that my sexuality was sinful, or at least undesirable, simply because it was unmentionable. No one ever talked about sex at church, and I for one was afraid to ask. Since my parents were Christians, I figured they probably wouldn't want to talk about it either.

Things really haven't changed that much in the last thirty years, even though the public schools have tried to pick up much of the slack in sex education. But because they often approach sex education in a value-free manner and treat it like an academic subject, they not only fail to answer the most important questions kids have about sex, but they actually make the subject boring. One fourteen-year-old boy described his sex education class at school as "all these dumb little books . . . I don't think they could teach me anything. Maybe how many sperm are in a drop of semen, but I don't even *want* to know that. It's not going to help me any."[13]

We cannot assume that parents are accepting the responsibility for teaching their children about sex. Most parents avoid talking to their kids about sex, even though they wish they could. The Search Institute study cited earlier found that although most parents believe that sex education belongs in the home, only one-third of the 8,000 adolescents surveyed reported that they had ever had a good talk with their parents about sex.[14] Another recent study found that 45 percent of America's teenagers say they learn "nothing" from their parents about sex. "Three out of four say it's hard to talk to their fathers, and 57% percent find their mothers tough going. Only about a third (36%) say they would ask their parents for any desired sexual information, while almost half (47%) would turn to friends, sex partners, or siblings."[15] The following paragraph, written by a twelve-year-old girl, is typical:

> My mother decided to finally have the talk with me. But I knew about that subject long before my mother told me about it. When she was telling me, she kept asking me if I had ever heard anything about that. I kept saying no, as if I had never heard a word. But you know how it is, everyone picks everything up on the streets. My mother wasn't the first one to tell me. Actually, she was the last.[16]

Nor can we assume that kids are learning all they need to know from other sources. Even in our present "age of enlightenment," there are many early adolescents who remain essentially uninformed and disturbingly ignorant concerning their sexuality and how their bodies are changing. A few years ago, for example, my wife and I took care of a one-week-old foster child, whose mother, we found out later, was fourteen years old. Incredible as it sounds, she did not even know she was pregnant until she went to the doctor with severe abdominal pains. It was only a few hours later that she gave birth to a six-pound baby girl.

Several years ago I asked over seven hundred junior highers in a survey, "Where do you get your information about sex?" Most answered, "School," but it is hard to know whether they meant health education classes at school or friends at school. The second and third most common answers were "friends" and "parents." Other typical answers were: "TV," "Myself," "By doing it," "On the streets," "I keep my ears open," "Wherever I can get it," "Nowhere," "Nobody gives me a straight answer." One girl replied, "I refuse to answer that question because it doesn't belong in the church."

It is revealing that although all seven hundred junior highers surveyed were members of church youth groups, only three kids indicated that they had received any information about sex from their church or church leaders. In the extensive *Rolling Stone* survey, "Sex and the American Teenager" (1985), there is no evidence at all that the church plays a role in the sex-education process or that religious instruction significantly influences sexual behavior.[17] This is very unfortunate when you consider that the best place of all for young adolescents to learn about sex is under the care and guidance of the Christian family, not from magazines, TV shows, friends, or "by doing it." God created our bodies, and he gave us our sexuality. The Bible has much to say about sexuality and intimacy. We need not be ashamed or embarrassed to talk about sex within the four walls of the church.

To the church's credit, many denominations and Christian publishing houses have recently developed a number of excellent Christian sex education programs.[18] Despite these new resources, it is safe to say that most church leaders, perhaps because they are afraid of controversy, are still reluctant to discuss the subject of sex with their young people except from a negative, moralistic, or judgmental perspective. The result is that kids get this message from the church about sex: "Sex is filthy, dirty, and nasty; save it for the one you're going to marry." Certainly, it is a confusing message and one that answers few of the questions about sexuality that teenagers have.

I am not suggesting that every church needs to conduct sex-education classes during the Sunday school hour, but it would seem appropriate and reasonable for youth workers, particularly junior-high workers, to let kids know that they can talk freely about sex in the church. Lightning won't strike if words like "vagina" or "masturbation" are said in God's house. Junior highers should be able to get straight answers to their questions from a Christian point of view. They are already getting answers from every other point of view.

Some people, especially parents, think that if they don't bring up the subject, then kids won't be concerned about it. They argue that talking about sex will only make kids more curious or overstimulate them and encourage experimentation. Fortunately, it just doesn't work that way. Experimentation is caused by a lack of information, not an abundance of it. Ignoring the subject doesn't make it go away. Sooner or later, usually sooner, there comes a time when kids must have the information they need concerning their bodies, and if they don't get it at home or at church or at school, they'll get it somewhere else.

Be Honest with Junior Highers about Sexuality

As I mentioned earlier, sex-education curriculum written from a Christian perspective is now available. It is not the purpose of this book to suggest a detailed junior-high sex-education program. I believe, however, that any attempt to deal with the subject in a junior-high group should be characterized by openness and honesty. Openness will allow all of the issues to be dealt with in a secure and nonthreatening environment. Honesty will insure that the kids get the "straight scoop" about sex in a helpful and assuring way, rather than getting half-truths, misinformation, and myths.

Besides dealing with the basic issues of puberty, one of the first steps in teaching sex to junior highers is to help them "unlearn" some of the myths that they have picked up about sex from the media and from other sources. It is truly amazing how much bad information kids have already learned by the time they are ten or eleven years old.

Here are just a few of those myths:

1. Sex is a big problem. Many kids believe that this is true because they hear so much about all the problems that sex brings. Every TV show is about problem love affairs, people getting venereal disease or AIDS from sex, and the like. They see all the how-to books and magazines and read the advice columns on how to overcome sexual dysfunction. Ads on the radio offer help for male impotence. Dr. Ruth Westheimer on her *Sexually Speaking* program discusses everyone's problems, no matter how bizarre they might be. Junior highers need to know that, despite what they hear in the media, sex is not a worrisome problem or a source of stress and anxiety for everyone. They need to know that there are in fact many people who have well-adjusted, enduring, satisfying, (and yes, exciting) sexual relationships within the bonds of marriage.

2. Sex is technique. Many young people believe from the books

71

and magazines they read (as well as from sex education classes in school) that sex is 99 percent technique, or *doing it*. They need to know instead that making love involves much more than learning the mechanics of sex. It involves the whole person—mind, body, and soul. It is a relationship that requires time and commitment.

3. Everyone is doing it. This is a very common myth among young people that kids themselves like to perpetuate. It puts a lot of pressure on young people who have not become sexually active because they feel left out. But the truth is that everyone is not doing it. We need to help kids understand that "it's okay to say no way."

4. Sex makes the world go round. Due largely to overexposure (literally) in the entertainment media, young people not only believe that sex must be the best thing there is, but the *only* thing there is. We need to help kids keep sex in its proper perspective.

5. You prove your manhood (or womanhood) by having sex. Many young adolescents, especially boys, believe that sexual prowess determines manhood. It might be a good idea to remind them that the world-champion copulators are not people, but rabbits and hamsters. Real men prove their manhood by accepting responsibility for their actions and demonstrating good judgment and self-control.

There are other myths as well—the idea that sex is a disgusting taboo or that sexual behavior has no consequences. These and many other issues need to be discussed with junior highers.

Before beginning with any kind of sex-education program in your church, be sure to plan ahead, decide what you are going to cover in advance, and discuss it with the church leadership and with the parents of the kids. It might be a good idea to actually go through the material that you propose to use with the parents so that they will know what you are going to do and give you the support that you need. You might want to think of other ways to involve parents in your sex-education program as well.

Regardless of what you do, be honest, open, and biblical about sex with your junior highers. Young adolescents are maturing sexually, and they have a natural curiosity about the subject. Let's not allow the media and the world to do our sex education for us by default.

TEACHING THEM TO TAKE CARE
OF THEIR BODIES

A final thought on physical development: As junior highers become more aware of their bodies and more concerned about their appearance and their physical development, it would be appropriate for youth workers in the church to show kids how proper nutrition and health care can be a reflection of their Christian commitment.

Traditionally, churches have shown a great deal of concern for people's souls but have not offered much help for their bodies. Since God gave us our bodies, creating each one in his own image, and since they are in fact a "temple of the Holy Spirit" (1 Cor. 6:19) and we are asked to "present our bodies" back to him (Rom. 12:1), it would be quite consistent with Scripture to help young people learn to care for their bodies properly.

This is of particular importance when it comes to what the early adolescent eats. Junior highers are true "junk-food junkies," and nutritionists are deeply concerned about the long-range effects of today's poor eating habits.

The Maternal and Child Health Service reports that the three groups most vulnerable to poor nutrition are infants and young children, adolescents, and expectant mothers. Another nutrition survey indicated that young people between the ages of ten and sixteen had the highest rates of unsatisfactory nutritional status, and boys more than girls. Problems included being underweight or undersize, obesity, iron-deficiency anemia, and dental caries.

It is generally agreed that nutrition hits one of its low points during adolescence.[19]

This is especially bad news when you consider that the adolescent growth spurt is second only to infant growth. The body is developing rapidly, including the brain, which is perhaps the most vulnerable to abuse. There is strong evidence that early malnutrition (in infants) directly affects intellectual competence, but little is known about how nutritional deficiencies affect the brain during later childhood and adolescence.

It would seem a logical and responsible conclusion, however, that to encourage good eating habits would be of critical importance at this age. You could be doing junior highers in your group a great service by raising their consciousness about this and other health issues.

5.
SOCIAL DEVELOPMENT IN EARLY ADOLESCENTS

With early adolescence comes a marked increase in social awareness and social maturity that parallels the many physical changes taking place. Relationships, especially with their peers, become very important to junior highers. When they were younger, they only needed playmates, but now they need and seek more meaningful friendships. Friends are the very lifeblood of adolescence; they are people who can be trusted, who listen, and who understand feelings.[1] Loneliness becomes a new experience for junior highers, and the fear of rejection becomes a source of anxiety and often dictates behavior patterns and value choices. Junior highers will usually do whatever is most conducive to making friends and keeping them.

In my surveys on junior highers, I learned that most junior-high students like school for one reason: School is first and foremost a place to be with friends. The reverse is also true. Those who strongly dislike school do so usually because their friends are not there or because "enemies" are present there. Teachers, curriculum, facilities, and the like play only a secondary role. The implications of this should be obvious for junior-high workers in the church. Youth groups should have a good amount of "redeeming social value" for junior highers to really enjoy being a part of them. The youth group should be a place where good friends are found.

THE DRIVE FOR INDEPENDENCE

To understand what is actually happening with junior highers in the social realm, we must begin with another stock theme of adolescent psychology. (By "stock theme," I mean that this is something you can find in practically every book on adolescent behavior, and this leads us to believe that it is common knowledge among experts in the field.) Simply stated, we can say that it is a primary task of early adolescence to break ties with the family and to attempt to establish an identity that is separate from parents or other authority figures.

Junior highers have begun to make the transition from childhood to adulthood; they possess a drive toward independence. They want to come up with an identity of their own, to be their own person, and to make their own choices and commitments, to be set free, and to be treated like adults. This is the age when kids become highly critical of their parents and consider them, and sometimes their values, to be hopelessly old-fashioned. They may be embarrassed by their parents and prefer not to be seen with them in the shopping mall or sit with them in church because they don't want anyone to mistake them for children. While there are certainly exceptions, this behavior is definitely the norm for early adolescents.

This naturally accounts for many of the problems between parents and their early adolescent children. Many parents are caught completely off guard by this. They find it hard to understand why they are suddenly "losing control"; they never had such problems before. Just when their children are finally learning to be good, obedient boys and girls, they become junior highers and appear to take a giant step backward. But it is always wise to remember that adolescent development progresses via the "detour of regression," and parents who understand this will find parenting junior highers a much less traumatic experience (although it is never easy).

Many parents may have an understanding of what is going on but are reluctant to allow it to happen. As their children move toward independence, they become more rigid and refuse to let out any rope. This results in clashes and strained parent-child relationships. Parents often need extra help understanding that their young adolescent child is not viciously turning against them. They need to know that the child is simply seeking autonomy, trying to discover and establish his own identity as an individual, and needs to be given opportunities to do so. This does not mean, on the other hand, that parents should take a *laissez-faire* or a "hands-off" approach; this would be even more disastrous. Parents remain the most important influence on children throughout their adolescent years. They should simply work *with* their children, nurturing them by giving them a little more freedom, responsibility, and trust, rather than "provoking them to wrath" while they are trying to grow up.

THE BRIDGE TOWARD INDEPENDENCE

The Peer Group

While it is true that the primary goal for the early adolescent is independence, it is also true that it is an impossible goal, at least for the time being. Junior highers do want to be independent, but the gap between the security of the home or parents and this sought-after independence is far too great. To charge out into the world on one's own is a pretty scary thing. Junior highers want to be treated like adults and to think for themselves, but they lack the confidence (and competence) necessary to take on the responsibilities that go with it. There needs to be a middle ground, a "bridge"— something to prepare them for independence and adulthood.

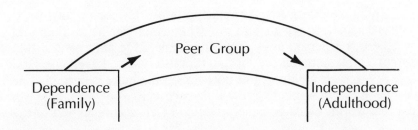

In today's society, this is primarily the function of the peer group. The stepping stone or bridge that links dependence with independence is a close alliance with and conformity to the peer group. It is ironic that for a junior higher to find his identity as an individual, he must lose his identity. As Joan Lipsitz says, "It is one paradox of adolescence that it is possible to achieve this inner, apparently singular, sense of individuality only when one sees oneself in terms of a larger social context."[2] That larger social context is the peer group. What the crowd does, he does. What the crowd likes, he likes. It seems just the opposite of independent thinking, a movement away from independence. This accounts for the many fads so characteristic of the junior-high years as well as the inevitability of cliques and associations that often seem so negative. But this conformity, strange as it may seem, is an essential part of adolescent development and helps junior highers gain the security and confidence needed for adulthood.

This is described by Howard and Stoumbis:

> In his desire for independence, the early adolescent appears to become a rigid conformist to the mores, dress, speech, and attitudes of his fellows. Security is found in identifying with the group insofar as is at all possible. If group standards denigrate strong academic performance, the high grades are for "squares" and "goody-goodies." The seventh-grade pupil who was a strong student becomes only an average ninth-grade student, which confuses and shocks his parents and teachers. The early adolescent is almost certain to develop an air, a manner of sophistication or pseudo-sophistication, which he hopes will cover up the worries, doubts, and feelings of uncertainty that are usually with him. During this time the early adolescent is highly susceptible to undesirable influences and individuals—if they are admired by his peer group. To gain status and recognition he must conform to these new standards. The role of the school should be obvious in developing desirable values, attitudes, and standards, and in providing socially approved experiences and situations.[3]

By conforming to the peer group, the junior higher is subconsciously trying to find out whether or not he is liked and accepted as a person away from the home. It is only natural that parents offer acceptance, love, admiration, encouragement, and security to their children, but now something more is needed. The early adolescent wants to know if he is equally okay "out there" in the real world. Once he is accepted and feels secure as part of the group, then he is likely to have enough confidence to step out and to experiment with being "different"—the discovery of his own identity. The peer group becomes in fact the bridge to independence.

Drawing from personal experience once again, I was very much like my parents, as most youngsters are, during my preteen years. My values, beliefs, and tastes where almost identical to those of my parents. I remember as a child listening to country-and-western music (and liking it!) because my mother and father did. I knew all the words to "Your Cheatin' Heart" and never missed the "Grand Ole Opry" program on television.

But sometime about the fifth or sixth grade, I noticed that other kids my age did not listen to country music, and for the first time, that had an impact on me. And so, much to my parents' dismay, through junior high and high school, I listened to the rock music of my era (remember the Coasters and the Shirelles?). Country music was for ignorant hillbillies (parents included), and there was no way I was going to be caught dead listening to it again. My father and I would fight for control of the radio whenever we got into the car. All the other kids liked rock and roll, and so did I. I was not being hypocritical, incidentally. I really did like rock music. But in retrospect, I know that I liked most of it because it was very important to like the same things my friends liked. To be different was to be foolish.

But as I recall, it was as a senior in high school and during college that I finally dared to leave the security of the crowd. By that time I had courage enough to strike out on my own and be a little different. I became a great fan of folk music, then bluegrass and country music. I came full circle, and for my parents it was like the return of the Prodigal Son.

That's the way it usually goes with early adolescence. The pattern is predictable enough to say that it is normal and necessary for junior highers to lose their identities to find them. Failure to conform (even when the group is doing something wrong) can produce feelings of guilt and inadequacy as severe as the feelings involved in going against one's conscience. Caught between a rock and a hard place, so to speak, the result is often a difficult struggle for the junior higher. This is what we usually mean by *peer pressure:* "Should I do what my friends want me to do, or should I do what I know is right?" He or she knows that either of the choices will lead to painful consequences.

The important thing for adults, particularly for parents, to understand is that this conformity to the peer group is not all bad. It is true that junior highers are very susceptible during this time; they can choose the wrong kind of friends and get involved in things we do not approve of, but the alternatives are usually worse. Better a little bad influence than no friends at all. There are a great many adults who haven't yet "grown up" or who are seriously maladjusted emotionally or psychologically simply because they were never able to fit in as adolescents. It is not uncommon to find adults still conforming to every whim of the crowd, hoping to find the acceptance they never received during their youth.

It is hardly ever helpful to junior highers for parents or youth workers to overreact to what must be considered an important part of adolescent development. In the church, it is not uncommon to use Scripture, such as "Be not conformed . . ." as a way of telling kids that they should not be like other kids or that they should only have "approved" friends. It is not likely that Romans 12:2 was intended to be interpreted or used in that way. Good or bad, acceptance by and conformity to the peer group is the chief method children use to socialize themselves into adulthood. In the words of educator Jerome Kagan, "The early adolescent . . . needs many peers to help him sculpt his beliefs, verify his new conclusions, test his new attitudes."[4]

It was not always this way. In civilizations of the past, it was not the peer group who socialized young people into adulthood. It was the adult community. As I mentioned in chapter three, it was common in many cultures for there to be "rites of passage" in which children at puberty were permitted entry into the adult world. From then on, the adults in the community no longer regarded that young person as a mere child, strictly under the care of their parents, but as a young adult, ready to become a part of the adult world. Adults gave them a place in society where they could learn the responsibilities of adulthood and receive a controlled introduction to adult life. In colonial America, for example, adolescents were given entry-level jobs in the community. Boys were given apprenticeships from age fourteen to twenty-one, girls from twelve to eighteen. Working alongside adults, they could learn a variety of trades, such as farmer, shipbuilder, barber, hatter, baker, and even candlestick maker.[5]

It is neither honest nor useful to romanticize or glamorize the past—there can be no denying, for instance, that adolescents were often badly mistreated in colonial America. Still, it is clear that historically adults played a much bigger role in the lives of adolescents than they do today. Certainly, down through history, there have always been peers, peer groups, and peer friendships. But they were never as predominant in the development of adolescents as they are today. Generally speaking, peers have virtually replaced the adult community as the primary "bridge" to adulthood. Where once adolescents learned how to be adults from other adults, they now learn about adulthood primarily from each other. This is essentially why "youth culture" exists (a relatively recent phenomenon, as most of us know). It is a place where kids can practice being adults. They practice on each other. It's kind of a miniworld, with its own customs, styles, music, dress, language, and so on. It is a middle ground between childhood and adulthood where kids can, as Erik Erikson would say, discover their self-identity.

Why has this change taken place? Why is it that adults no longer involve themselves in the lives of teenagers as they once did? One obvious answer to that is that we don't live in the same kind of world we once did. We no longer live in a rural, agrarian society like the one our forefathers knew. Instead, we live in an industrialized, technological society, which puts many new demands and a great deal of pressure upon adults. As a result, today's adults have little time or energy to devote to "other people's kids." The sad truth, in fact, is that in today's world many *parents* hardly have time to devote to their own kids.

Psychologist David Elkind has written extensively about how adolescents are negatively impacted by these changes in modern society. In his book *All Grown Up and No Place to Go*, he says this:

> In today's society we seem unable to accept the fact of adolescence, that there are young people in transition from childhood to adulthood who need adult guidance and direction. . . . In a rapidly changing society, when adults are struggling to adapt to a new social order, few adults are genuinely committed to helping teenagers attain a healthy adulthood. Young people are thus denied the special recognition and protection that society previously accorded their age group. . . . Young people today are quite literally all grown up with no place to go.[6]

Another Way: The Role of Adults

There are many people who believe that the role of the peer group that I have just described is so universal as to be considered one of the unchangeable laws of nature. For many years, I too, was convinced that, like puberty itself, God designed the process of passing from childhood to adulthood via the peer group. But did he?

I began to question this after considering several individual junior highers who had experienced some rather serious problems trying to "fit in" with their peers. In one case, for example, a young adolescent boy with a great deal of potential had fallen in with the wrong crowd, committed a serious crime, and ended up in a juvenile detention facility to serve a ten-year sentence. In another case, a fourteen-year-old girl attempted suicide after she was rejected by some of her peers. If, as adolescent psychologists tell us, "having friends" is the natural, normal way for kids to make the transition from childhood to adulthood, why are there so many problems associated with it? Why do so many bad things happen?

I don't believe that the psychologists and sociologists are incorrect about the peer group's importance. It *is* vitally important. But I believe that this is true primarily because in today's society there is *no other way* for young people to navigate safely the waters of adolescence. Young adolescents need *someone* other than their parents to whom they can turn for companionship, friendship, guidance and, as Kagan puts it, to help them sculpt their beliefs, verify their conclusions, and test their attitudes. The peer group is the place where such a person can be found.

That is not to say, however, that willing adults cannot still have a marked influence on the adolescents they know. In fact, it's happening all around us. As powerful as the peer group has become in the lives of adolescents, most of today's young people are still hungry for something more.

Studies have shown that throughout early adolescence, young people continue to look first to their parents for advice and guidance on important issues. Not only that, but parents also remain the primary models for their adolescent children. While the influence of peers increases dramatically during early adolescence and the influence of parents decreases, the influence of peers never completely outweighs the influence of parents.[7] This, of course, should be good news for parents who might be led to think that they no longer have any significant influence on their adolescent children.

But next to parents, who or what influences young people the most? Over the last couple of years I have asked numerous people a similar question: "Who, besides your parents, had the greatest amount of influence on your life when you were a teenager?" Almost always, the answer I hear is the name of an adult—a teacher, a coach, a neighbor, a relative, a pastor, a youth worker, an adult friend. Rarely, if ever, does anyone mention the name of a *peer-group* friend. In light of the belief that the "tyranny of the peer group" has such a powerful influence, this seems odd to me. In fact, it has led me to believe that perhaps peers actually rank third in the "influence pecking order." While there can be no doubt that the peer group plays a vital and important role in the development of today's teenagers, I believe that kids still look to "other adults" for help and guidance, even though there are few "other adults" willing to accept that role.

This may explain why young people are so susceptible to celebrity worship—why they make heroes out of rock stars, movie stars, and other popular personalities who have made themselves available for adoration and emulation. In most cases, these are adults who appear to identify with adolescents, who understand them, and who are, by adolescent standards, successful. They are not always young; rock star Mick Jagger, for example, is in his forties. But with the absence of "real-life adults" who care about kids, people like Jagger are there to fill the vacuum.

I believe that while our earlier diagram showing the peer

group to be the primary bridge from childhood to adulthood is an accurate description of the world that we live in, we must add the fact that "other adults" play an equally significant role.

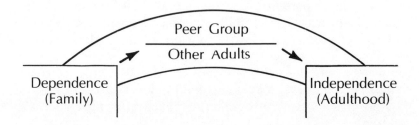

The bridge to adulthood is a relational bridge. Junior highers need people other than their parents who will help them to mature and to become independent. They need many friends—peer friends, yes, but also adult friends. Most junior highers I know are thrilled when an adult other than their parents takes them seriously, listens to them, and affirms them in some way. Such an adult is given a great deal of power and authority over them because they are so special and rare.

I am thankful that, when I was a teenager, there were a few "other adults" who cared about me. Even though they were few (I can count them all on the fingers of one hand), they were extremely influential in my life. I know that I am a youth worker today because there was a youth worker twenty-five years ago who took a special interest in me.

This analysis helps us to understand why youth ministry in the church is so important. Youth ministry connects adults and teenagers. It is not just a program "for the kids by the kids." It is not the creation of a "youth ghetto" in which a youth pastor is hired to give the young people "something of their own" and keep them out of the adults' hair. Instead, youth ministry should find ways to get the young people *into* everyone's hair.

Some youth workers have instituted a program in their churches called "Adopt an Adolescent" in which they invite all of the adults in the church to voluntarily "adopt" one of the teenagers in the church for a period of one or two years. The adults commit themselves to remembering their young person in prayer, welcoming them each week to church, honoring them on their birthdays, visiting them, inviting them to their homes or to family outings. The result of such a program is the fostering of positive and lasting relationships between the youth and the adults of the church. It's a simple but effective way to help adults assume the responsibility for the youth of their church and community.

Youth ministry today must be much more than games and fund raisers and weekend retreats. It must get adults involved in the lives of teenagers in a positive way. There may come a day when the junior highers in your group will ask themselves the question: "Who, besides my parents, has had the greatest influence on my life?" Let's give them plenty of good people to choose from. In today's world, when so few adults seem to care about the well-being and healthy development of teenagers, it is indeed refreshing to find people in the church who are willing to invest themselves in the lives of teenagers. That, I believe, is God's way.

FRIENDSHIP: THE TIES THAT BIND

Allowing Them to Choose Their Own Friends

One of the great fears parents have is that their adolescent children will become part of the wrong crowd. And usually their fears are justified. It is very easy for junior highers to choose friends who do not hold Christian values and who may exert a negative influence on them. Young people who smoke, drink, use drugs, or involve themselves in other kinds of negative behavior are sometimes in the majority on a typical junior-high campus. It is natural to want to protect our children from this kind of behavior, if possible, and to encourage them to choose the right kinds of friends.

But we cannot choose their friends for them. They must have the freedom to make their own choices. We can and should offer guidance, but it is usually destructive in the long run to criticize or to put down the friends that our junior highers select. To do so is to attack their judgment and to show little or no faith in them. When it is apparent that there are some dangers inherent in a particular relationship, then it should certainly be discussed, but we must never assume that antisocial behavior is always contagious. Psychologist Eda Le Shan offers this advice:

> There are times when it is a necessary part of growing up to live through a particular relationship. Much growth and learning about oneself can take place, even in some of the most ill-advised friendships.
>
> The only real protection against poor friendship choices is whatever help we can give our children in respecting themselves so much that they are unlikely to choose relationships that will hurt or demean them, and that we help them to understand enough about human motivation and behavior to judge others with insight.[8]

Two developmental issues are at work here: (1) junior highers need to learn to make decisions on their own and (2) junior highers need to have friends. It just makes good sense to allow junior highers to choose their own friends. When we do, there is a much better chance that we will remain one of them.

Also, we need to remember that as young adolescents most of us made some poor choices of friends, and somehow we survived. Chances are pretty good that today's kids will, too.

Choosing Between Friends and Faith

Junior-high ministry can be very rewarding. Early adolescents, who are trying to think for themselves and make meaningful commitments on their own, are often very open and responsive to the message of the gospel. Unlike older teens and adults, junior highers have not become rigid, skeptical, or hardened toward spiritual things. This makes them very reachable without manipulation or coercion. I have seen hundreds of junior highers choose freely to follow Christ.

But junior highers, young Christians that they are, are rarely able to put much of their faith into practice right away, especially if it means putting their friendships in jeopardy. They are not ready to sacrifice their friends for their faith. As was stated earlier, friends are the very lifeblood of adolescence, and they are crucial to adolescent development. If a choice must be made between friends and faith, they will choose their friends nearly every time. Faith can come later. ("When I'm an adult, then it will be easy.") Having friends is the most important thing now.

What this means for the junior-high worker is that it is rather foolish to force kids to choose between friends and faith if it can be avoided. Many times we do this without even realizing it. For example, when we ask them to make certain kinds of public stands (like witnessing), we are indirectly asking them to make a decision. The junior higher tends to think: *If I do it, the kids will think I'm some kind of a nut—a Jesus freak!*

I led weekly Bible clubs at several junior-high schools when I was a Youth for Christ staff member early in my youth-ministry career. Most of these clubs met after school, usually at a church or home within walking distance of the school, and they were reasonably well attended. But there was one club that did not have a convenient meeting place near the school. I had to use a church bus to pick up the kids after school.

Each week when the school day was over, that old red and white bus (with "First Baptist Church" painted all over it) would be parked in front of the school. At the time, I had no idea why only two or three kids showed up. Dozens of kids at the school had said they wanted the club, but when it came time to get on that bus, they were nowhere to be found. In retrospect, I know that I was asking for the impossible. To get on that funny-looking church bus in plain view of all their peers would have taken a lot more courage than most adults are able to muster.

It takes a great deal of boldness to be able to stand apart from the pressure of the crowd. And boldness takes time to acquire. Junior highers should not be made to feel they are less than fully Christian because they fear being different. They will have many opportunities during their lives to stand up for their faith and to move against the flow of group pressure, but these opportunities should come as a natural result of their growing Christian commitment. As junior-high workers, we are better off helping kids to understand the meaning of their faith rather than forcing them to make impossible choices. When we know why we believe, we are able to make wise decisions.

On the other hand, junior highers can be encouraged to share Christ with their friends, invite these friends to church or to the youth group meeting, get involved in service projects, and make all

87

kinds of public stands, so long as they feel reasonably secure doing so. It's not an all-or-nothing proposition. Every group and every individual is different, and you as the junior-high worker must be sensitive to each person's needs and level of maturity. But generally it's best to avoid situations that might be excessively threatening to the early adolescent. There is no need to push them too hard.

Breaking Up Cliques: An Exercise in Futility

The clique is probably the most prevalent social structure of early adolescence. A clique is defined by Webster as "a narrow exclusive circle or group of persons." Eric Johnson defines it as "a small group of friends who stick together and shut others out."[9] While cliques are certainly not limited to junior highers, they do seem to take on great importance during the seventh, eighth, and ninth grades and cause a great deal of concern for junior-high workers and teachers. Ideally, we want to foster a feeling of unity within the group, with each person expressing openness and friendliness toward everyone else, but that is very seldom attained in junior-high groups. Even though most junior highers themselves regard cliques as unfair and wrong, they can't seem to avoid them. They are a major part of the social life of the adolescent; they help in the transition from dependency on the family to the many upcoming associations outside the family. A junior higher would probably define the clique that he or she is a part of as "my best friends."

A common question asked by youth workers in the church is "How can I break up the cliques in my junior-high group?" The question arises naturally, since it is generally acknowledged that cliques are not desirable and should be eliminated if possible. For a long time I had difficulty coming up with an answer that would satisfy me, let alone anyone else. I, like most junior-high workers, have never had much success at breaking up cliques. I finally came to the conclusion that it was essentially useless and basically a mistake even to try. Good or bad, cliques are here to stay and are just a necessary part of growing up. They must be considered a given of early adolescence, and the junior-high leader will have to work around them, rather than against them.

It is possible, however, to reduce the destructive or negative aspects of cliques in the junior-high group. One way is to provide as many opportunities as possible for group interaction and participation. Whenever the group or class is doing something together—mixing, playing games, talking to each other—relationships between cliques and individuals are more likely to improve. But when kids come to a meeting or activity in their cliques, stay in their cliques, listen to or participate in the program in their cliques, and then leave in their cliques, there is little chance that conditions will improve. Rather than lecture on the evils of cliques, it is best to involve the kids in a variety of activity-centered learning experiences that require communication and cooperation with each other, as well as in group games, and other chances to relate to those outside their little cliques.

Most people of all ages find new friends by accident, not by design. You can't tell someone to stop liking one person and start liking someone else. You don't create community and unity by having little buzz groups and hand-holding sessions (although it *has* happened). Community and friendships develop usually as a by-product of something else. If a group of kids puts on a play, goes on a long trip, or participates together in a service project, chances are good that cliques will be reduced and that community building will happen almost automatically.

It's also true that small group projects or activities *in which the group is allowed to choose its own members* serve to encourage or strengthen cliques. Small groups work fine with junior highers, but it is usually best to use a random selection process to determine group members or to assign kids to groups not entirely made up of their close friends.

Watch for Those Who May Be Rejected

Within any junior-high group there are usually a few kids who just don't seem to fit in. While this is not a problem for most junior highers, there are some who have real difficulty making friends and finding acceptance from others in the group. They may be rejected because of their appearance, personality, where they live, what school they go to, what their family is like, their abilities, interests, mannerisms, language, or perhaps just because they are new. The list of reasons a person might be excluded from the group can be endless, and they are undeniably unreasonable to the adult. Even though junior highers may seem cruel to each other, they are merely being typically junior highish: They have discovered that one way to satisfy their own need to feel accepted or superior is to find someone else whom they can look down on, ridicule, or simply ignore. If a junior higher can identify someone else in the group as a "nerd" or a "loser," then that makes him or her look superior by comparison. It's a rather sinister, although normal, way for a young person to build self-esteem. But it's a sad thing for the young person who is the object of this kind of discrimination—as most junior highers are at one time or another.

No junior-high group should allow a situation like this to exist unchecked. You as a junior-high worker should always be on the lookout for those in the group who appear to be rejected and try to help them to fit into the total group. While you can't force people into being well-adjusted and having friends, doing nothing is usually not the best alternative. Kids should be made aware that one of the things that sets the Christian community apart from the non-Christian community is that no one is shut out. Everyone is accepted, regardless of how the world sees things. That has always been an identifying mark of the Christian.

Some junior highers who are rejected are quite capable of living with the situation without any sign of trauma or despair, and they may appear to accept their roles as loner with ease. We should, of course, be supportive and thankful for them. But that is usually not the case. Most young adolescents who have no real friends in the group and who are unhappy will, given the opportunity, simply leave and seek acceptance elsewhere. Those who, for whatever reason, must stick it out will more than likely have a very difficult time, and there may be long-range damage to their personality, faith, and ego development. We should do whatever we can to find out why a person is being rejected and, whenever possible, provide help.

A few years ago in one of my junior-high groups, an eighth-grade girl was being shunned by the other girls (and boys) in the group. It was having a negative effect on her, so we youth workers decided to see if we could help. We discovered that her parents had been divorced for some time and that she lived with her father, who had never remarried. One result of this was an apparent lack of guidance in personal hygiene and other social graces that are important for young ladies emerging into womanhood. One of our female counselors was able to spend quite a bit of time with this girl and helped her considerably. Of course, acceptance did not instantly occur just because she smelled or looked better, but gradually she did grow more comfortable as barriers between her and the others in the group were broken down. Her self-image began to improve as well.

There are no easy answers here, and the example above is not intended to be a model for similar situations. But the sensitive junior-high worker will give special attention to kids who need it and will find creative ways to discourage the natural tendency for junior highers to discriminate against those who may be a little bit different. We can help by getting kids involved with each other more and by allowing needy kids to get more recognition by being allowed to do the things they do well. Sometimes it just means that we must be an especially good friend to every person in the group, thus becoming a common link between them all. Perhaps in us they can see Christ, the one who is able to make us all one.

6.
INTELLECTUAL DEVELOPMENT IN EARLY ADOLESCENTS

> When I was a child, I talked like a child, I thought like a child, I reasoned like a child. When I became a man, I put childish ways behind me. (1 Cor. 13:11, NIV)
>
> Paul

A real key to understanding junior highers is to take seriously the fact that early adolescence is a time of transition from childhood to adulthood, in more ways than one. Physically, the body changes so that it can function as an adult. Socially, we have seen how the junior higher makes the transition from dependency to independency via the bridge of relationships. And while these definitive shifts are taking place in the physical and social areas, the young adolescent is in a period of equally exciting and disturbing intellectual change.

There are basic structural differences between the way a child thinks and the way an adult thinks (as the apostle Paul has pointed out in the passage quoted above), and once again, we find that it is during the junior-high years when most young people begin to develop adult understanding. The brain shifts gears, so to speak, and a whole new world emerges, much more complicated than before, yet wonderfully exciting. Prior to the age of eleven or twelve, a child's understanding of reality is largely tied to what he or she can experience. But a qualitative change occurs coinciding with the onset of puberty, and this is more than just becoming more intelligent or learning more. The junior higher develops the ability to reason more logically, to conceptualize, to think abstractly, and to move from one abstraction to another. He can speculate on the many possible effects of something he wants to do. He can keep a lot of "ifs" in his head at one time and yet come up with an answer. These are all things he was unable to do when he "thought like a child."

PIAGET'S THEORIES OF COGNITIVE DEVELOPMENT

In recent years, a variety of theories have been postulated about how the brain develops. But not all of them have survived close scrutiny. For example, in the late 1970s two researchers, Herman Epstein of Brandeis University and Conrad Toepfer of the University of Georgia, described in several journal articles what they called the theory of "brain growth periodization." In effect, this theory said that brain growth increases during certain periods of life and conversely decreases—the brain stops growing—during other periods of life. During the periods when the brain is growing, it can absorb new information. When it is not growing, no new information can be absorbed. This theory caught my attention because one of the "no growth" periods identified by Epstein and Toepfer was early adolescence, from twelve to fourteen years.[1]

A theory like this one may offer a reasonable explanation for why junior highers seem to be uninterested in learning algebra or American history, but it does not explain the inquisitiveness and seemingly unquenchable curiosity of this age group. While the theory of brain growth periodization received a great deal of attention when it was first introduced, it has since been discarded by most developmental psychologists as having little or no substance.[2]

The most widely accepted research in the field of cognitive development (how the mind develops) has been done by the late Jean Piaget, a Swiss psychologist. He conducted numerous studies over a period of several decades and made brilliant observations of the thought processes of children, especially of their ability to think logically. He noted that intelligence, whatever that may be, does not increase at a steady rate, but in spurts. Therefore, the conventional IQ score often is not an accurate measure of intelligence because people shift from one "stage" of thinking to a higher "stage" at different ages. This theory has significant implications for the junior-high worker.

Piaget's stages of cognitive development are levels of thought, each one more sophisticated than the one before. People move from one stage to the next, never backward, as they mature. Piaget called the first stage the *sensori-motor* period. It is best characterized by infants who do little or no organized thinking. They merely respond. Their perception of the world is obtained directly through their physical senses. By about age two, the child has learned that actions have physical consequences and that he and his environment are not the same.

The second stage is called the period of *pre-logical* or *pre-operational* thought and lasts typically from ages two to five. The thinking of children during this stage contains a magical element— they are not able to distinguish well between events or objects they experience and those they imagine. Although things are beginning to make sense, their point of view is still that everything in the world revolves around them. Language and other symbols develop at this stage.

The third stage is called the period of *concrete operations*. (An "operation" is defined as a logical thought process.) Here children are not as ego centered, but they still relate most things to themselves. Children between the ages of five and twelve are usually in this group. They learn to observe, count, organize, memorize, and reorganize concrete objects and information without losing the distinction between the real and the imaginary. They can figure things out for themselves and solve problems. The mind is much like a computer at this stage, processing information and making conclusions based on concrete data. It is during the stage of concrete operations that children attend "grammar school" and are given many opportunities to use this ability. They learn facts and figures, the parts of speech, the names of all the presidents, how to read and write, multiply and divide, and so on.

The fourth (and final) stage is called the period of *formal operations*. Most people enter this stage between age eleven and age fifteen if they are going to enter it at all. Piaget discovered that some people never do. But when a person does reach stage four, he or she is able for the first time to deal with abstractions, to reason, to understand and construct complex systems of thought, to formulate philosophies, to struggle with contradictions, to think about the future, and to appreciate the beauty of a metaphor. Put another way, this stage gives one the ability to perform operations on operations, that is, to classify classifications, combine combinations, and relate relationships. One can "think about thought" and at the same time develop an awareness that knowledge is extremely limited.[3] This incredible new power to think is usually acquired during early adolescence—the junior-high years.

The shift from stage three- to stage-four thinking is much like getting a color television set after having only known black and white all your life. A brand new dimension is added to a person's ability to think. David Elkind calls it "thinking in a new key" and he reminds us that it doesn't happen overnight.

> It is important to remember that young people are as unfamiliar with their new thinking abilities as they are with their newly configured bodies. Moreover, thinking on a higher level takes time to get used to. Teenagers need to become accustomed to living in a new body. And just as they are often awkward in the use of their transformed bodies, they are sometimes equally awkward in the use of their new thinking powers. As adults, we have to be careful not to mistake their awkwardness in thinking, which may sometimes manifest itself in the form of insensitive remarks, for anything more sinister than inexperience.[4]

Graphically, Piaget's stages of mental development might look like this:

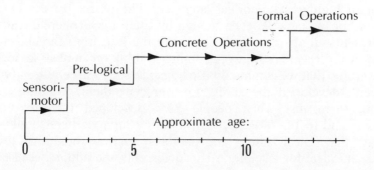

Recognizing the Differences

The differences between a stage-three mentality and a stage-four mentality are what is significant for the junior-high worker in the church. These differences have a profound effect on education and ministry in the church generally as well. It is interesting that, according to studies, many Americans never reach adolescence in their capacity to think.[5] They never learn to think abstractly, so they never reach the stage where they reexamine their world, the people in it, what they believe, and themselves. It is important to know this because to require a person who has not reached the period of formal operations to think in abstractions is to require the impossible.

This is one of the reasons children and most young adolescents find it very hard to listen to a sermon. Sermons are boring not because the pastor is a boring speaker (although that may also be the case); instead, the sermon is boring because it consists mainly of stage-four (abstract) concepts, which only those people who have made the shift from concrete to formal operations can understand. Even if a child, or any person who had not made the shift to formal operations, were listening intently, he or she would probably not fully grasp the meaning of what was being said.

Many pastors will include a "children's sermon" somewhere in the church service to alleviate this problem. It is intended to communicate with children on their level, the level of concrete operations. Unfortunately, a common mistake that is made in children's sermons is the use of object lessons and parables that require formal operational thinking. Object lessons and parables contain highly metaphorical language. The object (in the object lesson) or the parable, even though by itself it is a concrete reality, represents an abstract truth. To make the leap from the object to what it represents requires the ability to think on an abstract level. It is ironic that we commonly use object lessons with children (who haven't developed the ability to appreciate them), and we stop using them just when people *have* developed the ability to understand them—at adolescence. Junior-high workers should be aware that object lessons and parables, such as those that Jesus told, are ideal for teaching early adolescents and adults because in most cases their minds are able to do the work necessary to understand them.

Similarly, it is important to realize that a person who has reached the stage of formal operations can become extremely bored when forced to limit himself to a lower level of thought. No real intellectual challenge is offered in the church where stage-four people are asked to memorize religious facts or to accept everything that is taught without questioning. Much of our Sunday-school curriculum is loaded with stage-three questions, such as "How long was Noah afloat in the ark?" rather than stage-four questions, such as "How could a God of love possibly destroy the earth's population at the time of Noah?" or "How could we learn from Noah's experience?" The latter question would probably frustrate stage-three thinkers but would be very stimulating for those in stage four. It is not sufficient merely to fill the heads of young adolescents with knowledge. They need to begin to put it into practice and to "learn about their learning."

Many junior highers will know a great deal about the Bible, or about religion and the church in general, but will have a difficult time relating it to anything else in a meaningful way. This period of transition from knowledge to application will most likely be troublesome for them. Here is probably one of the biggest problems with the traditional practice of "confirmation," which is done in many churches during early adolescence—seventh or eighth grade. Junior highers attend confirmation classes and are asked merely to learn and then to give back information: "Question: What is the First Commandment? Answer: The First Commandment is 'Thou shalt have no other gods before me.'" Once they have "learned it"—the beliefs and dogmas of the church—and acknowledged an acceptance of it, then they are confirmed. Too often these are nothing more than rote memorization classes that ignore the young person's need to question and to come up with a faith that is his or hers.

Joseph Adelson, a political scientist, made an observation concerning young adolescents that is pertinent to spiritual training.

> Just as the young child can count many numbers in series and yet not grasp the principle of ordination, so may the young adolescent have in his head many bits of political information without a secure understand-

ing of the concepts which would give order and meaning to the information.[6]

Just as in political science, there are concepts essential to Christianity that must be understood to make it meaningful; for example, love, ethics, morality, justice, freedom, sacrifice, trust, faith, hope, compassion, the future, and so on. These are stage-four concepts; they give order and meaning to the religious knowledge previously acquired as a child. As a young person grows older, and the mind develops, these begin to come into focus. If they do not, or if they are withheld, there is no question that the young adolescent will lose interest altogether in religion and, more specifically, in Christianity.

The Questioning of the Early Adolescent

As adolescents move from stage-three to stage-four thinking, they commonly begin to question much of what they have been taught in the past. Their new capacity for thinking things through and coming to their own conclusions makes it necessary to reaffirm the learning they acquired from their parents, teachers, and peers. They want assurance that it is really true. They will often spot inconsistencies and contradictions that they hadn't seen before, or that, at least, didn't bother them before.

Jerome Kagan cites the following example:

The fourteen-year-old broods about the inconsistency among the following three propositions:

(1) God loves man.

(2) The world contains many unhappy people.

(3) If God loved man, he would not make so many people unhappy.

The adolescent is troubled by the incompatibility that is immediately sensed when he examines these statements together. He notes the contradictions and has at least four choices. He can deny the second premise that man is ever unhappy; this is unlikely for the factual basis is too overwhelming. He can deny that God loves man; this is avoided for love of man is one of the definitional qualities of God. He can assume that the unhappiness serves an ulterior purpose God has for man; this possibility is sometimes chosen. Finally, he can deny the hypothesis of God.[7]

Despite the oversimplification, this example is typical of how early adolescents privately work out their own set of values and beliefs. They have been told that sex (for them) is wrong, yet they find pleasure through sexual experiences. Is pleasure therefore wrong? They have been told that God answers prayers, yet they prayed and nothing happened. Why? Many junior highers are dismayed to find themselves facing an endless stream of problems like these that force them to make some adjustments regarding beliefs they hold at the moment. Left alone, the adolescent grows more and more skeptical, assuming that all religious truth is nothing more than wishful thinking. Sometimes this leaves the adolescent temporarily without a commitment to any belief.

These major conflicts pivot on the fact that old assumptions are challenged by new perceptions—perceptions created by the transition from concrete to formal operations. It is difficult to pinpoint when this shift occurs, but it is generally agreed that age has much to do with it. It has been said that the ideas of a twelve-year-old German, for example, are closer to those of a twelve-year-old American than to those of his fifteen-year-old brother.[8] But while this may be generally true, there are, of course, slow developers, fast developers, and those who don't develop at all. This places an additional responsibility on the junior-high worker because the transition from stage-three thinking to stage-four thinking normally occurs during the early adolescent or junior-high years. It is likely that there will be, in the same junior-high group, kids who are radically different from each other in their intellectual abilities. This is normal and to be expected.

The most obvious implication for the junior-high worker is that junior-high ministry must be very personal. This adds weight to the importance of building relationships with individual kids and getting to know them well. This doesn't mean that junior highers must be individually tutored, nor does it mean that they cannot be challenged with levels of thinking they are unaccustomed to. It does mean, however, that the junior-high worker will be aware of kids who are having difficulty understanding certain concepts or who show an apparent lack of interest or seem bored. Likewise it is not necessary for one to become an "answer man," providing instant answers to every question. It is necessary, though, to be someone who is willing to listen and to encourage their questions. They need someone who will share their struggles.

KOHLBERG'S STAGES OF MORAL DEVELOPMENT

Another set of stages that we pass through on our journey from childhood to adulthood has been identified by Lawrence Kohlberg, a psychologist at Harvard University. He expands on Piaget's theories, but with an added emphasis. His concern is with moral reasoning—how people think about right and wrong, truth and falsehood, good and bad. Kohlberg is interested in the "why" of moral reasoning, not just the content or the "what." People often arrive at similar conclusions or decisions but for completely different reasons. Kohlberg found that people go through fixed, predictable stages of moral reasoning, which explains how they arrive at moral decisions. This process is very similar to Piaget's stages of cognitive development. Kohlberg also found that we all grow through stages in a fixed sequence, and we never skip a stage. But we do proceed at different speeds, and most people stop at a particular stage and proceed no further.

Kohlberg maintains that one's moral development can be seen (or measured) according to changes in (1) one's concept of justice—right and wrong, (2) one's ability to see things from another's point of view, and (3) the value one gives to human life. Each of these change as one progresses up the moral development ladder. Kohlberg identifies three *levels* (major divisions) and six *stages* (subdivisions).

Kohlberg designates a "Stage O" that is devoid of any moral reasoning. Practically, it applies only to infants, who simply know that "What I want and like is good." *Level one* (Preconventional) is entered by the child at around age two. This level is typified by actions that occur without regard for others. All acts on this level are based on self. "Life" and "things" are not easily differentiated. At level one there are two stages: *Stage one* is based on whether it will hurt me. If I am frowned at, scolded, or hit, I don't do it. If I am rewarded, praised, or patted on the head, I do it. *Stage two* is the "What's in it for me?" stage—what some would call, when it occurs in adults, the Playboy philosophy. Fun is whatever turns you on; people can be used for your own benefit. There is a sense of fairness in sharing, but it is based on how it will benefit me. This stage lasts usually up through age ten, but some people never go beyond this stage. Others regress to it from time to time, such as when undergoing stress.

Kohlberg's Stages of Moral Reasoning	Typical Age
Stage 0: Good is what I like	0 to 2
I. Preconventional Level Stage 1: Avoid Punishment Stage 2: You be nice; I'll be nice	2 to 6 6 to 10
II. Conventional Level Stage 3: Good boy, Good girl Stage 4: Law and Order	9 to 13 11 to 15 up
III. Postconventional Level Stage 5: Democracy, conscience, voluntary agreements Stage 6: Truth; Sacredness of life as a universal value	adolescence (about 14) up rarely shown; fullest moral maturity

Kohlberg's *second level* (Conventional) differs from the first in that here people submit completely to outside authorities, stereotypes, rules, and traditions. Again, there are two stages included here: *Stage three* is the "way I'm supposed to be." You do what the group considers right. Conformity to the wishes of the group (especially peers) is the norm. Good and bad is defined by the culture or by "society." Many junior highers are at this stage. *Stage four* is "law and order." What's right is what's legal. Law and morality are the same thing here. Obedience to rules or some outside authority is important. This stage is usually entered at adolescence, but it includes most adults in America as well. Many Christians (including pastors) are solid stage-four people and probably will be for the rest of their lives.

The *third level* of moral reasoning (Postconventional) is based on what Kohlberg calls a "principle morality." Those who enter this level do so through a process of questioning the accepted rules and working out for themselves moral principles they hold to on the basis of their own convictions rather than because of some authority. According to Kohlberg, only about 20 percent of the population ever attain this level. Again, there are two stages: *Stage-five* people would say that society is an instrument of man rather than the other way around. The majority rules; law still fits in, but it can be changed if society considers it unjust. No one is better than anyone else, and each person has a responsibility to others. *Stage six* is Kohlberg's highest level of moral reasoning—stage-six people are very rare. "Truth" is the determining factor in all decisions. Decisions are based on what is universally, logically, and ethically right. Justice is based on the interests of the least advantaged person in every situation. Human life and dignity are sacred human values. Kohlberg identified Jesus Christ, for instance, as a stage-six person.

So how does all this relate to junior-high ministry? It is certainly not my intention in presenting Kohlberg's stages that you attempt to categorize people into this stage or that, or that you try to turn all your junior highers into full-fledged "stage sixers" by the end of next year. What is of relevance is that we need to be aware that the mind develops in an orderly fashion, not haphazardly, but according to a God-given pattern. Even those who disagree with Kohlberg on the specifics of moral reasoning will probably agree on that point. One stage of thinking comes before the other and one leads to the next. The mind of the junior higher is not simply an empty jar waiting to be filled with knowledge, but it is itself growing in its capacity to assimilate information and to reason. Nor can you turn young adolescent minds into adult minds overnight. But we can be a vital part of the process by giving kids opportunities to nurture and to stimulate their growing minds. According to Kohlberg, it is only through struggle, through challenge, through constant testing and reevaluation of old beliefs that people continue in their ability to think and to make morally responsible choices. There is no place to go but up.

Secondly, it is significant that Kohlberg's stages closely parallel Piaget's. It is impossible, for example, for people to pass beyond Kohlberg's stage-four morality, that of law and order, until they have moved into Piaget's period of formal operations, when abstract thinking and a high level of questioning is possible. An understanding of this becomes very helpful when ministering to young people who are at different points of intellectual and moral development.

ADOLESCENT RELAPSE

While both Kohlberg and Piaget have given us what appear to be smooth patterns for intellectual development, there are snags, especially when we are talking about junior highers. Some people have suggested that Kohlberg should have included in his system a "stage 4½" to accommodate what is often referred to as "adolescent relapse"—a giant step backward that occurs shortly after the onset of puberty.

It would seem logical that with newly acquired mental capabilities, junior highers would be anxious to excel academically and to put their improved brain power to work, but the opposite is often true. It is a fact that for most young people the quality of schoolwork goes down, not up, during the early adolescent years, and this is true in Christian education as well. Kids who may have performed very well during the prejunior-high years often do quite poorly when they reach adolescence, much to the dismay of parents and teachers alike. This poses a frustrating problem for junior-high workers, and this is yet another reason why some people avoid working with this age group altogether.

As I see it, there are two primary reasons why adolescent relapse is normal and to be expected. The first has to do with the emergence of the major distractions described earlier: the sudden physical growth, the rapid sexual development, the readjustment of relationships with adults and peers, and the quest for autonomy. There is a lot going on in the life of the early adolescent, to say the least. To expect a smooth academic performance when such turmoil is going on is to expect the impossible. It is not easy to make intellectual pursuits (Bible study, for example) fascinating enough to prevail over these urgencies. It is often not until the tenth, eleventh, or even the twelfth grades that many young people develop a driving intellectual curiosity and a pleasure from dealing with ideas. This makes designing junior-high curriculum a real challenge for everyone involved.

A second cause of adolescent relapse has to do with motivation. Junior highers are not sufficiently motivated to perform at a high level academically. They are, in fact, "between motivations." When they were younger they were motivated to do well in school because it pleased their parents. They would bring their papers home from school (with good grades on them) and their parents would proudly display them on the refrigerator door. This motivated them to continue to get good grades on their schoolwork. When they get older, they will again be highly motivated by a desire to be better equipped for adulthood, to get a good job, or to expand their knowledge on a particular subject. But during the early adolescent years, they are in between these two motivations. They are neither motivated to please their parents, nor are they motivated to prepare themselves for adulthood.

So, how do we motivate junior highers, particularly about spiritual matters? There are no easy answers, but here are some suggestions that may increase the *chances* that the junior highers in your group will be interested in what you're doing.

1. If it is, in fact, other urgencies that distract junior highers from concentrating on academic, intellectual, or spiritual things, then make these other urgencies part of the curriculum. In other words, make it relevant. Kids will always be more interested in things that relate to where they are, what they are going through, and so on. If the subject matter has no practical application, it may be a complete waste of time. (See pages 134, 135.)

2. Variety is important. Active, growing minds become bored easily. Use a variety of approaches and methods to cover a variety of topics. Don't use the same approach week after week after week. Surprise the kids once in a while; give them something to look forward to.

3. Involve kids in the learning process. Use as many activity-

centered learning experiences as you can. Avoid lecturing when teaching can be done some other way. (See chapter 9.)

4. Create a warm, friendly atmosphere in which learning can take place. If kids feel right away that they are accepted, that they are in a place that is fun, exciting, and happy, then motivation is not so great a problem.

5. Keep it personal. If each person knows that he or she is important, special, and cared for, and you are a friend, he or she will be motivated to please you, not disappoint you. It is usually the kids who feel left out who are least motivated to participate and to learn.

7.
PSYCHO-EMOTIONAL DEVELOPMENT IN EARLY ADOLESCENTS

"I don't know why I cry so much and why I get so upset over things. Sometimes I think I'm getting younger, not older."

Thirteen-year-old girl

By adult standards, junior highers are very emotional people. Because they have acquired the ability to think in a new way, they also have acquired the ability to *feel* in a new way. They have brand new emotions, which are extremely intense and completely unpredictable. Junior highers have been known to giggle uncontrollably during the first part of a youth meeting and then become angry or despondent during the second half. And this occurs for no apparent reason. While this kind of behavior could be classified as typical, it is important to understand that there really is no such thing as a "typical junior higher" when it comes to emotions. It is possible to have within a group of fifteen to twenty junior highers those who are boisterous and loud; others who are quiet and shy; still others who might be fearful, or self-critical, or confident, or depressed, or on and on. Emotionally, there are myriad peaks and valleys for the junior higher. As if riding on a rollercoaster, they run the gamut of emotions and moods before they begin to settle into a pattern, usually later in adolescence.

Like the other areas of life that we have discussed earlier in this book, psycho-emotional development has much to do with the transition from childhood to adulthood that is taking place during the early adolescent years. More accurately, psycho-emotional changes are the *result of* changes taking place in all of the other areas. The child approaches the early adolescent years depending on the mind, body, and social systems that have supported him for eleven or twelve years; then, as if by magic, much that he has come to depend upon begins to change. His body begins to grow and develop; his friends and interests outside the home begin to compete with the security previously found in his family; his view of the world begins to change as his mind develops; and then he finds that his emotions begin to "flip-flop" like Mexican jumping beans. The young adolescent's once stable world suddenly feels like it's made out of Jell-O.

Unfortunately, the word *emotion* suggests agitation and excitement. There is often a tendency to think of emotions as strange forces mysteriously arising from the depths to seize the person and place him at their mercy. This extreme view exaggerates the dramatic and disturbing aspects of emotions and fails to acknowledge that much of the emotional life of a junior higher is calm and constructive. A person can be quite emotional without flying into a rage, crying hysterically, or being silly. Emotions are always present in one form or another, no matter what behavior we are displaying at the moment.

Emotional turmoil may exist in early adolescents primarily because there is turmoil in the physical, social, or intellectual areas of life as well. Emotions are not foreign intrusions; they are more or less a reflection of what is going on generally in one's life, as well as a reflection of one's maturity. They hardly exist apart from these contexts. This is one of the reasons that it is practically impossible to make any predictions about how a group of people will integrate their emotions with their behavior (especially junior highers), since each person responds to situations and circumstances in his or her own way. One person may go through a great deal of stress in a given situation, while someone else may have no difficulty at all. Such is the case with junior highers. There are some early adolescents who seem to be sitting on an emotional powder keg, while others are able to take most everything in stride and show an unusual amount of emotional stability.

Even though emotional development is actually a secondary characteristic of junior highers, their emotional inconsistency and unpredictability cause a good deal of concern and frustration for parents, teachers, and youth workers because a junior higher's emotions are likely to be translated into some kind of action. In other words, they don't hide their emotions very well, even though they may try to. If a junior higher is feeling lousy, he will more than likely let you know in some "creative" way, and perhaps he will attempt to make everyone else around him feel lousy, too. This tends to make life interesting, to say the least, for the junior-high worker, and it also tends to make any kind of meaningful ministry among this age group extremely difficult, if not impossible, *unless* the emotional characteristics of junior highers are known and taken into consideration by those doing the ministry. Let's take a look at a few of those characteristics.

THE PSYCHO-EMOTIONAL CHARACTERISTICS OF ADOLESCENCE

Emotional Intensity

The emotions of early adolescents are very intense. There really is no middle ground, no halfway mark. People, events, and things are either one extreme or the other—it is the best thing that ever happened or it is the worst. A thing is either superior beyond compare or so inferior as to be worthless. Many events and problems take on an importance out of all proportion to their actual significance. Broken romances, failure to make the team, or poor grades may result in depression so great as to lead to suicide. Suicide, by the way, has become the number two killer of teenagers in the United States today, with eleven- to fourteen-year-olds representing a significant part of that statistic. Some five thousand adolescents take their lives each year, and for every one adolescent suicide, there are fifty to one hundred attempts.[1] Other common symptoms of emotional distress in adolescents include eating disorders, such as anorexia nervosa, insomnia, truancy, delinquency, drug or alcohol abuse, and complete withdrawal.

Emotions are intense during early adolescence primarily because they are new. As a junior higher gains an adultlike way of thinking, he also gains adultlike emotions, which are unlike those he had as a child, and it takes him awhile to get used to them or to control them. Therefore, when a junior higher is feeling good about something, he is very often ecstatic about it. When in love, it is greater love than anyone could possibly understand. As an eighth grader in love, I remember plastering my bedroom walls from floor to ceiling with my girl friend's name, and writing her name over every square inch of my schoolbooks, homework papers, desk tops, tennis shoes, ball gloves, and anything else with space enough to write. Of course, when we "broke up," I was heartbroken and wept bitterly, but it didn't take too long for someone else to take her place.

So it goes with the emotions of junior highers. Unlike older, more mature teenagers, they fail to cope with their feelings realistically or consistently; instead, they tend to surrender to them.

The emotions of a junior higher can be explosive as well as deep. At times, their discontent with themselves and others will express itself in anger, and that anger is likely to be expressed physically rather than the verbal expression manifested by older adolescents. If something happens that the junior higher doesn't like—a person may bump into them or call them a derogatory name—they may lash out and throw a punch. Junior-high and middle schools deal with considerable fighting between students, with the girls often being just as violent as the boys. Anger against adults often expresses itself in outbursts that end in tears—anger not as focused as it is in high-school students. The anger of the junior higher is highly emotional and usually short-lived. It is also quite difficult to deal with. You can't reason with an angry, tearful girl or boy. It's best just to be understanding and wait it out.

Because of the intensity of their emotions, early adolescents are highly susceptible to emotional appeals. They are fascinated by whatever triggers a deep emotional response. Of course, this makes them a prime audience for TV shows and films that play on emotions. They also like listening to music that is highly emotional, whether it be frenzied rock-and-roll or heartrending love songs. Junior highers may also be lured into drugs or mysticism because of their emotional power.

The temptation for the junior-high worker in the church is to take full advantage of this when attempting to produce desired results. You can get junior highers to do almost anything if you get to their emotions. If you can make them feel guilty, afraid, excited, ecstatic, angry, or whatever, you can usually elicit the desired response. But like emotions themselves, these responses are usually very shallow and temporary. Emotions are not only intense at this age, they are also transient, and anything based on them is also going to be fleeting.

This is not to say that emotions are wrong or that they should be discouraged or restrained in the church. On the contrary, young adolescents need to have positive emotional experiences that come from personally encountering God. Emotions will always enter into the picture whenever a young person responds to the gospel, but it is neither fair nor wise for us to play on those emotions or to manipulate them emotionally. Be careful that invitations to accept Christ as Savior, to dedicate one's life to Christ, to volunteer for Christian service, and the like are presented without undue emotional pressure that may lead to only surface commitments.

Similarly, we need to let kids know that faith in Christ is not dependent upon our emotional condition at the time, despite the fact that junior-high faith is an emotional faith. (See page 132.)

Pseudo-stupidity, the Imaginary Audience, and the Personal Fable

Adolescent psychologist David Elkind of Tufts University has done much to help us better understand why junior highers act and feel the way they do. Drawing from the work of Piaget, Elkind has identified and named several characteristics of adolescent behavior stemming from the shift from concrete to formal operations. In his view, Piaget's work and theory have just as much to do with the affective domain (how one feels) as the cognitive (how one thinks and learns).[2]

The first of these Elkind calls *pseudo-stupidity*, the tendency to interpret and respond to situations in a much more complex manner than is warranted. While everyone does this to some extent, it is most common in young adolescents. The obvious seems to elude them. In trying to find a sock or a shoe or a book, they look in the least obvious places. In school, they may approach subjects at a much too complex level and fail, not because the tasks are too difficult but because they are too simple.

When young adolescents make the shift to formal operational thinking, they become capable of holding many variables in mind at the same time, of dealing with contradictions, possibilities, ideals, and propositions, and of comprehending metaphor and simile. But they do not yet have these new abilities under control. The capacity to weigh many different alternatives is not yet coupled with the ability to assign priorities and to decide which choice is most appropriate. Consequently, young adolescents often appear to be stupid when, in fact, they are too bright.

They seek complex, devious motives in the behavior of their friends, teachers, parents, brothers, and sisters for the simplest or most accidental occurrences. A simple discussion with a junior higher can become extremely complicated and sidetracked by the young adolescent's overeager intellectualization of the issue at hand. This results in miscommunication, misunderstanding, frustration, and, more often than not, hurt feelings.

Delia Ephron offers a good example of pseudo-stupidity in her book *Teenage Romance*. What follows is a conversation between a mother and her teenage daughter:

It's Saturday night and your mother is insisting that you be home by midnight:

"Oh, Mom, come on. Nobody gets home that early, nobody! Do you want me to be the only kid in the entire group that has to leave early? The only one who can't stay out? Do you? Do you want me to ruin everybody else's time because I have to leave because my mom doesn't trust me while everyone else's mom does? Is that what you want? Is it? Great, just great. You're really getting impossible, you know that? You've changed, Mom, you have. You never listen, you never try to understand. You just give orders—do this, do that. . . . You never let me do anything I want. Never. If you had your way, I'd be in jail. You know, you're ruining my life. Probably no one will ever invite me anywhere again as long as I live. I'll probably never have another date. I'll spend the rest of my life in my room."[3]

Another characteristic of young adolescents made possible by the advent of formal operations is what Elkind calls *the imaginary audience.* It is this characteristic that accounts for the young adolescent's extreme self-consciousness. Formal operations enable young people to think about other people's thinking. This new ability to think about other people's thoughts, however, is coupled with the inability to distinguish between what is of interest to others and what is of interest to the self. Since the junior higher is primarily preoccupied with his own self, he assumes that everyone else has the same concern. Young adolescents believe that everyone in their vicinity is thinking about what they themselves are thinking about, namely "me." They feel like they are constantly on stage, and that everyone is as concerned with their appearance and behavior as they are. They surround themselves with an imaginary audience.

This is another reason why young teenagers will spend so much time in the bathroom bathing and combing their hair. When they stand in front of the mirror, they imagine how everyone else will see them and what they will think. Everyone does this to some extent, but with junior highers, it is commonly obsessive.

The imaginary audience also helps to explain why junior highers feel such a need to show off, or to engage in disruptive or destructive behavior. In many respects, such behavior is really a performance. When a young person commits an act of vandalism, for example, he is probably thinking more about the reaction of the audience than he is about destroying property.

Fortunately, imaginary-audience behavior tends to decline with age as young people come to realize that other people have their own problems and concerns. But until then, the imaginary audience is very real indeed. Elkind suggests that we can help kids learn to differentiate between their own concerns and the concerns of others by taking a "middle-ground" position. If a junior higher says that nobody likes him, for example, it would do no good to tell him that people do like him. Instead, it would be better to say, "Well, I like you. And frankly, I can't understand why others wouldn't like you, too. What do others say or do that makes you feel that way?" This approach helps kids to test their feelings against reality and to see the world as it really is.

A third characteristic of early adolescent behavior is what

Elkind calls *the personal fable*. This is a form of self-centeredness that says, "I am a special case. I am unique." Indeed, young people *are* special and unique, but the personal fable distorts reality to the point that the young person sees himself as immune to the things that happen to other people. "Others will grow old and die, but not me; others will get pregnant, but not me; others will get hooked on drugs, but not me." The personal fable is an untrue story that young people tell themselves about themselves.

This is why it is often futile to talk to junior highers about the consequences of their behavior because they don't believe those consequences will actually happen to them. They believe that they will always be the exception. When kids get into accidents, get pregnant, get involved with drugs and the like, they do these things not because they have chosen to accept the consequences of their actions, but because they never thought those consequences would happen to them.

Another example of the personal fable is the teenager who says, "You don't understand me. You just don't know what it feels like!" The young adolescent perceives that his feelings and needs are so unique that they are beyond the realm of anyone else's understanding, especially adults'. Sometimes this can make communication with a young person difficult, particularly when you are trying to let him know that you *do* understand.

Elkind suggests that the best thing to do is to accept young people's points of view and to encourage them to check their versions of reality against that of others. He also suggests that rather than argue with them or deny them their perception of themselves, we should instead help them to see that other people are special, too. This approach helps them to distinguish between the ways in which they are like others and the ways in which they are different.[4]

None of these three characteristics—pseudo-stupidity, the imaginary audience, nor the personal fable—are by any means new. On the contrary, what makes them so interesting to us is that we recognize them right away. But by describing and labeling these characteristics of adolescent behavior, Elkind helps us to be more empathetic and less judgmental with junior highers. It is a common tendency in human nature to attribute the worst possible motives for behavior that we don't understand. Hopefully, by gaining insights such as these, we can deal with kids much more calmly and rationally, without an undue sense of moral outrage. If we recognize that such behavior is due in large part to the intellectual immaturity of early adolescents, not because they are "dumb," selfish, or insensitive to others, then we can be more mature in how we respond to the kids in our youth groups who exhibit such behavior.

Trial-and-Error Personality Development

While there are many generalizations that can be made about early adolescent development and behavior, perhaps the most accurate one is that the emotions of junior highers are unpredictable and difficult to make generalizations about. Emotional unpredictability helps to set junior highers apart from the rest of the human race. Adults and little children can normally be put into categories without too much difficulty: "She's such a pleasant little girl."; "Mr. Jones is a real happy-go-lucky sort of guy." Junior highers, on the other hand, may be pleasant today and holy terrors tomorrow. I have had kids in my junior-high groups who were unusually cooperative and enthusiastic one week and unexplainably belligerent and disruptive the next. I've also observed aggressive hostility and childlike submissiveness in the same meeting from the same junior higher. The young person who is talkative and open one moment could suddenly clam up altogether. Some people might wonder if these kids might be victims of some strange form of schizophrenia, but they are just being junior highers.

These strange shifts in mood and behavior are not limited to individuals; they are also found in groups. It is not uncommon for the dynamics in a group of junior highers to change from one week to the next. A particular lesson plan or program idea may be a smashing success on a given date with a given group of junior highers, but it could have been a complete flop if you had used it a week or a month earlier. It all depends on the mood of the group. With most junior-high groups, I have always had more concern (before a meeting, class, or social event) with how the kids were going to be (or how they would respond) emotionally than with how many would show up or with how good the program or the curriculum might be. There was always the fear that the group might be on a "downer"—uncooperative, on the defensive, or just plain nasty. As I have said before, it makes life interesting for the junior-high worker.

Adolescent psychology offers a reasonable explanation for this bizarre behavior, and this may be of some consolation. It certainly helps us understand what is going on, even if it doesn't alter the situation much. The explanation is this: In the process of adolescent development, junior highers are essentially "trying on" different personalities for size to see which one or ones fit them best. They will express a variety of emotions, feelings, attitudes, and temperaments to discover the range of reactions they get from others, especially their peers. If the reaction is favorable, the behavior may be repeated; if it is not, the behavior may be discontinued. This explanation may be an oversimplification, but it does help us to get a handle on what's happening. It is consistent with what we know about the primary tasks of early adolescence. Young people are making a transition from childhood to adulthood, and each one is trying to come up with an identity of his or her own. The personality, like the body and the mind, is being shaped during the junior-high years, and it is probably in its most unstable period.

This is why it is not at all unusual for the early adolescent to be an extrovert one day and an introvert the next. He is only trying to see what he will be most comfortable with as an adult. A junior higher may try all sorts of personalities—the class clown, the tough guy, the brain, the teacher's pet, the quiet type, the spoiled brat, the flirt—before his or her own distinctive personality traits begin to emerge. He has not yet committed himself to a particular pattern, but he will be doing this only a few years later in most cases. If a junior higher gets positive feedback from others by acting a certain way, this behavior will no doubt be continued. Conversely, negative feedback will usually act as a deterrent. Keep in mind, however, that negative feedback from an adult may very well be interpreted as positive feedback to a junior higher.

115

Obviously, this tends to complicate things when you are trying to encourage or discourage particular kinds of behavior. The whole process is, in fact, a natural form of behavior modification.

By the way, the junior higher is never really aware of this subconscious trial-and-error personality-shaping process. He doesn't wake up in the morning and say to himself, "Yesterday I tried my warm and friendly personality; today I'll see how my mean and nasty one goes over." It's not an overt kind of behavior; it is all quite involuntary, normal, and necessary.

HOW SHOULD WE RESPOND?

Now that we've looked at some of the psycho-emotional characteristics of early adolescence, it's time to consider what implications those characteristics have for our ministry among junior highers. How should we respond? Three significant considerations are that we should be building their self-esteem, we should be responding to our junior highers with patience rather than panic, and we should be exercising discipline, when necessary, wisely and appropriately.

The Adolescent's Struggle with Self-esteem

The most pressing psychological task of early adolescence is to build self-esteem. As I mentioned earlier, the number-one question on the minds of junior highers is "Do you like me?" They want to know if they are accepted by others, if they are okay. During early adolescence, they really aren't too sure. This is another indication that they are growing up, that they are making the transition from childhood to adulthood.

When a child is young, he or she has few self-esteem problems. Parents generally shower their children with praise and make them feel like they are the only children in the world. This is as it should be and provides security and safety for the child. But as the youngster approaches adolescence, he realizes that the security of the home and the security of the world are two different things. As he begins to seek independence and autonomy, and as he ventures forth from the protection of his home, he wants to know if he is going to be liked out there in the real world as much as he was liked at home. He also needs to discover whether he will have what it takes to survive on his own.

Bill Wennerholm has identified a number of steps that young people must take to build their self-esteem and to become healthy adults. They are part of a gradual process that usually takes several years. They include: (a) the establishment of emotional and psychological independence from parents; (b) the achievement of a separate personal identity; (c) an ability to motivate oneself and set one's own goals and direction; (d) development of one's own values and beliefs; (e) the ability to be in intimate reciprocal relationships; (f) the establishment of an appropriate sexual identity, which includes accepting and appreciating one's own unique body; and (g) the ability to function in a work capacity.[5]

The best way to help the junior highers in your group build self-esteem is to let them know that you do indeed like them and want to be around them. This is one of the reasons why relationships in youth ministry are so important—they help young people build self-esteem and feel good about themselves. It is also important to let kids know that you believe in them and take them seriously. One of the most effective ways to do this is to listen to them. When you give a junior higher your attention by being a good listener, you let him know that what he has to say is important and you value him as a person.

Another excellent way to help early adolescents build their self-esteem is to say something positive to them whenever you can and to avoid putting them down or making fun of them. Be liberal with praise. Catch them doing something good and let them know that you noticed. Most junior highers I know are so used to being scolded, nagged, criticized, and ridiculed that they think they have a sign on their back that says, "Kick me, I'm a junior-high kid!" Compliment your junior highers whenever you have the opportunity. Mark Twain once said, "I can live two months on one good compliment." Junior highers need to be complimented more often than that. And when you do compliment them, it is best to emphasize positive character traits rather than possessions or appearance. "I really appreciated the way you helped out last night," rather than "That's a great-looking shirt!" And don't hesitate to compliment them in front of other people, especially their parents. Even though they may act uneasy and embarrassed, down deep inside they are taking their bows and basking in the glory of it all.

We can also help young adolescents build self-esteem by giving them meaningful responsibility and opportunities for success. The second most important value to junior highers (the first is "to make my own decisions") is "to do something important with my life."[6] Joan Lipsitz of the Center for Early Adolescence has said that junior highers are "omnipotent in imagination, but impotent in action." They are extremely idealistic when they are young and have a keen desire to do something important with their lives, but they have few opportunities to do so. As a result, they become discouraged and they begin to believe that they are, in fact, incompetent and useless.

Most adults consider junior highers to be too immature and too irresponsible to do meaningful work. This is why there is virtually no job market for them. On the other hand, junior highers are the nation's baby-sitters. Almost every eleven to fourteen-year-old earns extra money by baby-sitting. The irony of this is that often the people who consider junior highers to be so immature and irresponsible are the same people who entrust their most prized possessions—their babies—into the care and safekeeping of junior highers. Either junior highers *are* responsible, or adults are acting irresponsibly by leaving them alone with their babies. I choose the first option. Junior highers are capable of accepting a certain amount of responsibility and they should be given every opportunity to "do something important with their lives." The same junior higher who won't pick up his dirty clothes off the bedroom floor will often jump at the chance to do something for someone else who needs work done.

There are literally millions of junior highers all over America who have nothing to do after school except to hang out, watch television, or get into trouble. Some of these are the "latchkey kids," who come home to empty houses because they live with one parent, both of their parents are working, or their parents don't care about them. These young people represent a tremendous mission field for junior-high workers who want to reach junior highers for Christ and make a significant difference in their lives. Churches could provide all kinds of meaningful after-school activities, such as mission and service projects, apprenticeships, volunteer work, and the arts, such as drama and music. I believe this is where the real cutting edge of junior-high ministry is going to be in the future: finding ways to effectively minister to young adolescents in the after-school hours.[7]

The Importance of Patience

As I mentioned earlier, this unpredictability in a junior higher's behavior pattern generates a good deal of anxiety for people who work with this age group. It is no easy task to adapt to the emotional ups and downs of junior highers week by week. It requires a considerable amount of patience, particularly when the behavior of the group is more negative than positive. The temptation in such situations is to punish them in some way, to give them a tongue-lashing, to call in their parents, or to threaten them with whatever might seem appropriate. In my experience as a junior-high worker, I can recall times of panic, despair, or anger, and my impulsive actions at such times did more damage than good. If you lose your temper, or overreact in a negative way, it rarely accomplishes much. Usually it only gives the group some helpful feedback that they will undoubtedly file away for future reference. (Now they know how to get to you.) There is nothing wrong with being firm and strict and being honest about your feelings, but they do need to see maturity and consistency in their adult leaders as much as possible. Junior highers demand almost superhuman standards from the adults around them.

Rather than losing control, it is best to try to be as understanding as possible and relatively good-natured through it all, even when the kids are angry, belligerent, or uncooperative in return. The best advice is to have patience, make as few demands on them as possible, and just wait it out. There really is no better alternative. Sometimes, when your planned program isn't going over with your junior highers and you've had just about enough of their sarcasm or rowdiness, it might be a good idea to "punt"—to

119

offer something that might be more compatible with the immediate mood of the group, rather than to force something on them they are not ready for.

Dr. William Sippel, a respected junior-high principal, gives some good advice about how to get along with this age group:

> It takes a person with certain qualifications. He or she must have patience. It takes an understanding of these youngsters. One must not overreact to their emotional manifestations, not get upset over them. . . . To deal with them, one should be emotionally tough, and yet have very humanistic qualities. If one of them tells you off, you have to be well-adjusted so that it doesn't make you feel insecure. They may accuse you of being funny-looking. If you have a long nose, they may yell that out. That could bother you.
>
> We need people who are emotionally tough enough not to be bothered, yet human enough so that the next day you can give them the human help they need—as if nothing had happened. That takes a certain personality, almost the same kind the youngsters show, in a way—they have a lot of emotion, but are willing to make amends the next day.[8]

Discipline

The emotional ups and downs of junior highers will often create a real dilemma for the adult worker who is trying to be patient and understanding, yet at the same time remain firm and in control. How does a person maintain order and exercise discipline in a junior-high group without being tyrannical or without alienating, humiliating, or hurting the kids? Obviously, there is nothing to be gained by passively allowing complete chaos to exist in a youth-group meeting or other activity. It is not usually in the best interest of the group to permit a few high-strung, disruptive kids to destroy a meeting or ruin a learning experience for others. A certain amount of discipline that is effective without being oppressive or counterproductive is necessary.

The question of discipline—how much, how often, and how to go about it—is usually a nagging problem for people who work with junior highers. Again, there are no easy answers, since every situation will require a little different approach. Also, each youth worker needs to have his own style, consistent with his personality and the personality of the group. When discipline is necessary, the important thing is to do it with consistency or with a predetermined standard that is fair, just, and understood by everyone from the very beginning. It should not seem arbitrary or impulsive. If kids have a good idea in advance that certain types of behavior will result in some corresponding consequence, they will not only try to avoid it, but also their dislike for the disciplinary action will be transferred to the "system" rather than to you personally.

This may mean that some basic rules should be established and everyone made aware of them in some way. For example, whenever I lead a discussion with a group of junior highers, I first lay down a few ground rules:

1. Only one person talks at a time.
2. Raise your hand if you want to speak.
3. If someone says something that you don't agree with or that you think is "dumb," don't yell, laugh, put them down, throw a tantrum, or pick a fight. Just raise your hand and you'll get your chance to express your opinion.

It's not advisable to have too many rules. Rules tend to sound negative, and they put a damper on things. In fact, the more rules you have, the more rules get broken, and the more discipline problems you have when you try to enforce all the rules! One of the best ways to establish a few basic rules is to allow the kids to help create them. Create a "youth-group contract" with the kids. At one of your meetings, announce or pass out a list of proposed rules that you have chosen in advance. (The more the better. It's good to include a few that border on the ridiculous, such as "No spitting tobacco juice on the floor.") Ask the kids for their suggestions as well. When the list is complete, divide the group into smaller units and have them decide which rules they want to keep and which they want to eliminate. They should keep those that they feel are fair, just, and necessary for the smooth running of the youth group.

Then have a discussion with the total group, with each smaller group sharing their conclusions along with their reasons. If you find that the kids have eliminated some useful rules or have kept some undesirable ones, you may express your feelings also. But the final decision should be left to a vote of the group. Usually they will do a very good job of selecting or modifying the rules they consider essential and will be willing to honor. When all the discussion is completed, then the rules can be listed on a sheet of poster paper or parchment (like the Constitution) and signed at the bottom by everyone in the group. It can be posted on the wall as a reminder that you now have a contract.

Of course, it may be necessary to add amendments as you go along, adding or dropping rules when the group agrees. Some rules may be more important than others. The idea is simply to predetermine standards for group behavior in advance, so that you are never accused of being a dictator when you must administer some disciplinary or corrective action. Usually this procedure is more appropriate with larger groups than smaller ones. Again, you should do what is best for your own group and what is consistent with your style of ministry.

Obviously, the next problem is what to do when someone is guilty of disruptive conduct or of compromising the rules. Do you make them stand in the corner or make them do fifty push-ups? Do you report them to their parents or kick them out of the meeting? Do you embarrass them or put them down in front of the other kids? Do you hang them by their thumbs? Or worse?

As a rule, I have found it best to handle these problems individually with kids who consistently cause problems. This is where some personal counseling and honest sharing is extremely worthwhile. I have rarely had problems with kids I have a good relationship with and have spent a lot of time with on a one-to-one basis. Because they value my friendship, they are less apt to disappoint me and put that friendship in jeopardy.

One group has what they call the "Ugly Card System." It works this way: Whenever someone breaks the rules or creates a problem, he is given one or more ugly cards, depending on the offense. These cards are much like traffic tickets, with predetermined penalties attached. One or two cards is usually a warning, while a third, fourth, or fifth might result in some form of punishment. A person might have to stay and clean up after the meeting or be sent to the "ugly room" (use your imagination) while the youth meeting is going on. On the other hand, there may be ways for kids to get rid of their ugly cards by doing some positive things rather than being punished. Some junior-high workers have found this approach to be effective, but it may not necessarily be the best way for you.

Here's another idea: When I ran junior-high camps at Forest Home Christian Conference Center (in Southern California), we sometimes used a discipline system called the "Mutt and Jeff System"—for reasons I'm not really sure of. At the beginning of camp, the basic rules were usually announced (usually only two or three) and campers were informed that if anyone could not abide by these simple rules, we would arrange for them to be taken home. When we did have a problem camper, someone in authority (like the camp dean) would sit down with the camper and counselor and tell him there was no alternative but to send him home.

After the camper became thoroughly convinced he was in deep trouble, the counselor would then become the camper's advocate and request that the camper be given a second chance, promising that the camper would change his ways. After some consideration, the camper would be granted a reprieve. Usually this resulted in an immediately improved relationship between the camper and the counselor and almost always a positive change in the camper's behavior. I was involved in more than thirty camps with close to five thousand kids; to my knowledge, we never sent anyone home.

Here are just a few important guidelines to keep in mind regarding discipline:

1. Don't expect perfection from your kids. In other words, let kids be kids. They are junior highers, not adults. Being a kid is not a terminal disease that needs a cure. It's perfectly normal behavior.

2. Avoid disciplining kids in front of their peers. While the temptation is great to make an example out of wrongdoers, the results are usually counterproductive. You don't want to humiliate the young person so much that you destroy them, nor do you want to give them the attention that they were probably trying to get in the first place. As I said earlier, try to deal with them on a one-to-one basis.

3. Look beyond the behavior to what is at the cause of the behavior. Perhaps the junior higher needs attention (give it to him in a positive way), has a low self-image (build him

123

up), or just needs something to do (get him involved). Some kids are just bored. Boredom is not really a discipline problem; it's really more of a programing problem.

4. Don't get mad and lose your cool, pout, threaten the kids, make them feel guilty, or call their spirituality into question. Remain calm and try to keep *your* emotions under control. Even in the midst of chaos, kids need to know that *someone* is in control. They need that stability.

5. Give your junior highers plenty of opportunities to "blow off steam." Give them a chance to talk, yell, run, be with friends, goof off, so that when it is time to settle down, they will be ready to do that. They need opportunities to use up some of their emotional energy.

6. Try to retain your sense of humor. If someone does something funny, at least try to smile (if you can't laugh). Learn to enjoy the humor in some of the things they do rather than get mad because it distracts from what you had planned. Some discipline problems are really immature attempts to be funny (granted, they usually aren't funny at all), and it is sometimes best to "play along" until you have their attention once again.

7. Learn to "roll with the flow." As I said previously, if the mood of the group is not what you expected, learn to shift gears and back off. Don't force the kids to be something they can't be at that particular time. Be sensitive to what the group can handle.

8. Finally, don't always be looking for trouble. If you expect something bad to happen, it probably will. Junior-high workers who worry a great deal about discipline problems are usually the ones who get more than their share. It's a chicken-and-egg situation. People who are more positive and don't seem to anticipate discipline problems find that they have very few.

Remember that discipline depends a lot more on attitude than on rules, systems, punishments, and enforcement. There is much more to be concerned about in junior-high ministry than enforcing rules and maintaining order. You can spend all your time doing that. It is wise to know what you will do when a problem arises, but it is never helpful to dwell on the negative when working with kids. Keep it in the background. When a junior higher needs to be disciplined, try to be as understanding and as helpful as possible. Punishment or revenge is strong medicine for most early adolescent misbehavior. Try to interpret the cause of the behavior and then decide (calmly) the action that you should take, if any.

BEHAVIOR THAT HIDES MORE THAN IT REVEALS

People always wonder how an experienced junior-high worker is able to function in what appears to be a state of total confusion. I can remember times when I would invite the pastor of our church to speak briefly to the total junior-high group, and invariably he would stand before the group and try to quiet the kids down and achieve total silence, but without much success. Frustrated, he would look over in my direction and expect me (plead with me) to *do* something, when really there was not much that I or anyone else could do. What he needed to do was to proceed and to ignore the ever-present stirring of the crowd. Despite all the noise, he would be heard, even though he might wonder how in the world that might be possible. Rarely can you tell how well you are communicating with a group of junior highers simply by noting the decibel level or by waiting to get positive feedback from the group.

Then there was the time I had spent several weeks studying and discussing the concept of Christian love with another group of junior highers. We particularly concentrated on what it meant to be the body of Christ and how as Christians we should care for and love each other, to strive for unity and harmony, and so forth. The kids were really into it, and I was confident that the way the group had responded to this material meant that our group was going to be the most loving, harmonious collection of junior highers in town. Unfortunately, it wasn't to be. Less than a week later, two of the dominant cliques in the group were at each other's throats again, so one half wouldn't even speak to the other half. It was all I could do to prevent an all-out war. Apparently our study about love didn't make a very deep impression on them, I concluded.

Naturally, when things like this happen, you begin to wonder whether you are getting anywhere as a junior-high worker or teacher. Normally, you hope that you see results reflected in some kind of positive behavior, but with junior-high kids, you just can't count on it. And it rarely has anything to do with how well or how poorly you are doing your job. Learning and growth in junior highers will be taking place even when their behavior seems to indicate otherwise. A junior higher's behavior will many times hide more than it reveals, so you can't really depend on positive behavior to measure your success, failure, or results. You will be disappointed when you do.

This is one of the reasons that junior-high workers need patience. I have been involved in youth ministry now for over twenty years, and every now and then someone will approach me with a statement like "You probably don't remember me, but. . . ." And they are usually right until they refresh my memory. It often turns out that this person was in one of my junior-high groups fifteen or sixteen years ago, when I was convinced beyond a shadow of a doubt that my efforts were a total loss. I am still humbled and amazed when one of these people expresses his or her gratitude for my ministry then and in some cases informs me that it was while in my group that he or she made a commitment to Christ that is still meaningful today.

8.
SPIRITUAL DEVELOPMENT IN EARLY ADOLESCENTS

No one is quite sure how it all started, but everyone thinks they know who started it. It happened during the morning worship service, shortly after the pastor invited the congregation to pause for a few moments of silent prayer and meditation. The organ was playing softly. Heads were bowed and eyes were closed. Suddenly there was heard a sort of muffled, choking noise, like someone trying to contain a cough. This was immediately followed by giggles, then snorts, and within a few seconds, like a wave, the first three rows of the church, occupied primarily by junior highers, were laughing hysterically.

According to one fourteen-year-old eyewitness, it started when "somebody cut the cheese," although he declined to identify the guilty party. Some believe that it was the same elder who tried to introduce a resolution at the next church board meeting to ban junior highers from all worship services where adults are present. "These children are not capable of understanding the things of God," he said. "They are not only irreverent, but they are spiritually incompetent."

Unfortunately, there are many who share the view that "spirituality" and "junior highers" are two terms that simply don't go together. They don't believe that it is possible for junior highers to be "spiritual." Is it? What can we say about the spiritual development of junior highers?

There is, indeed, such a thing as junior-high spirituality, and there is much that can be said about it. It has characteristics, for instance, that can be listed and described.

1. It is a faith in transition.
2. It includes doubt and disbelief.
3. It is personal.
4. It includes feelings.
5. Junior highers have trouble putting it into practice.
6. It includes failure.
7. It is idealistic.
8. It needs models.

In this chapter, we'll take a look at each of these characteristics and discuss the church's appropriate response.

JUNIOR-HIGH FAITH IS A FAITH IN TRANSITION

The spiritual dimension of life cannot be set apart from the rest of life as if it were an entity unto itself. It is not. One's faith touches every area of life—the physical, intellectual, social, and emotional. This is why we have devoted so much space to these four areas so far. The "whole gospel" affects the whole person, not just the soul.

As we have seen, junior highers are changing a great deal during early adolescence in every area of life. They are, in many different and important ways, making a once-in-a-lifetime transition from childhood to adulthood. They are making the same transition in the spiritual area of life as well.

When we talk about spirituality, we are talking about one's relationship to God. And like most other relationships (a marriage, for example) spirituality has both an intellectual and an emotional component. Intellectually, it is necessary to understand what the relationship is all about, who the relationship is with, why the relationship is important, and there must be a commitment to that relationship. Emotionally, there are feelings that accompany and validate the relationship. These feelings can be described with words like love, passion, affection, romance, infatuation, adoration, devotion, joy, and ecstasy. Most marriages require that a couple feel "romantic love" at least once in a while to be successful, but they also require a healthy dose of intellectual commitment to their spouse and to the concept of marriage itself. Likewise, one's spiritual life is both an emotional experience (feelings) and an act of the will (beliefs).

To assess spiritual development in junior highers, then, it is helpful to pay particular attention to how junior highers *think* (intellectual development) and how junior highers *feel* (emotional development). If we understand that junior highers are in the process of making a transition in life both intellectually and emotionally, then we will have a better understanding of early adolescent spiritual development. Junior highers are indeed making a spiritual transition that parallels the changes that are taking place in these other areas.

JUNIOR-HIGH FAITH INCLUDES DOUBT AND DISBELIEF

When junior highers were younger, they had a faith that was simple, almost mythical—one that provided clear-cut answers to life's most difficult questions. It provided them with invincible heroes of the faith to admire and to emulate. They believed because their parents and their teachers believed. But now, with the advent of adulthood and the ability to think on an adult level (Piaget's stage of formal operations), they sense that the faith of their childhood will no longer suffice. They don't want to be embarrassed by what they believe. Instead, they need to develop a more mature kind of faith, one that is personal and makes the transition from childhood to adulthood along with them. Unless the church is willing to help junior highers discover this faith, it is in danger of losing them. Many junior highers reject their faith and lose interest in the church because they are still being asked to believe in a God whom they have literally outgrown. It is important, therefore, to help junior highers see God in completely new ways and to see how their faith in Christ relates to the new world that is opening up before them.

With their newly acquired ability to think, junior highers will naturally begin to doubt and to question the faith of their childhood. Some young people find it necessary to discard this old faith altogether, rather than modify it or try to live it long enough to understand it more fully.

For others, faith in God is weakened by a growing mind and a newly acquired world view that discredits anything that cannot be empirically proven or does not make "good sense." They see their old view of religion as a world of make-believe, and like many once cherished childhood myths, it is at least temporarily cast aside.

Of course, there are always a certain number of junior highers who will have no doubts whatsoever (no serious ones anyway) and who will remain absolutely faithful throughout their early adolescent years, and for them we can be thankful. These young people will simply build upon the foundation of their childhood faith. Still, they will need to modify their old beliefs and to increase their understanding of them. There will also be quite a few who have nagging doubts about their faith but are afraid to express them. This group is probably larger than the faithful. Early adolescents generally lack the self-confidence necessary to express these feelings openly, so they tend to keep them locked inside.

It is good to be aware of the doubts of your junior highers and to know why they may be experiencing pangs of disbelief, disinterest, or skepticism. But there is no need to attempt to eliminate their doubt. We can help junior highers by letting them know that their doubts and questions are permitted, that they are normal, and that God approves of them. Doubt is a necessary part of one's spiritual development. As Frederick Buechner once wrote, "Doubts are the ants in the pants of faith; they keep it alive and moving."[1] Even John the Baptist expressed doubts about Christ when he was imprisoned for his faith (Matt. 11:3). Kids need to know that while they may doubt God and find Him confusing and distant at times, God never doubts them. Sensitive youth workers will try to provide an environment of safety where junior highers have the freedom to be open, to ask questions, and to mine their faith for answers that make sense to them.

This is another reason why relationships are so important in junior-high ministry. Junior highers need a person, not a program, to whom they can turn with many of the questions and problems that they are struggling with in their lives. They need someone in whom they can confide, an adult friend who understands and who cares enough to listen. They need someone who will take their questions and ideas seriously without criticism. In most cases, parents are unable to fill this role. The solution to doubt is not necessarily better curriculum, more weekend retreats, confirmation classes, or a special youth-week commitment service. You can get a lot more mileage out of just being a friend.

JUNIOR-HIGH FAITH IS PERSONAL

David Elkind has suggested another result of the young adolescent's newly acquired thinking abilities: Religion changes from an activity (going to church) to a belief system—a personal faith. Because of this, junior highers tend to reject institutional religion, which is social, in favor of a personal faith, which is private.

> . . . but teenagers, who value their privacy—now that they have discovered that they can live in secret in their heads—and who are afraid that their secrets might be found out, discover that a personal God is a most trustworthy confidant. He won't squeal.[2]

Some junior highers may turn their backs on the church as a way of expressing their need for autonomy. In a way they are saying, "I'm not a kid anymore. I don't believe in that stuff anymore." It's part of the process of breaking free from parental and religious authority and the baggage that goes along with it. It usually has little to do with religion itself. The actual pros and cons of the gospel seldom enter into it. Young adolescents simply want to be able to make their own decisions about things like religion, so they may temporarily hang up entirely the faith that they inherited from their parents. This does not mean that they don't have a personal belief in God; they just don't see a need to express it outwardly. In fact, recent surveys have revealed that 95 percent of early adolescents believe in God, and that 75 percent pray "every day."[3] In such cases, there is no need to panic. Elkind suggests patience: "In general, most young people return to the faith of their parents once they become young adults and particularly when they become parents."[4] Scripture puts it another way: "Train a child in the way he should go, and when he is old, he will not turn from it" (Prov. 22:6, NIV).

We can be most helpful to young people who have temporarily

discarded their faith by loving them and taking their need for a sabbatical from institutional religion seriously. You can't force kids to attend church or to accept the doctrines and beliefs of the church. But you can provide an atmosphere of acceptance and friendship, and opportunities for them to discover Christ in a fresh, new way.

JUNIOR-HIGH FAITH INCLUDES FEELINGS

As we discussed in chapter six, junior highers are also experiencing adultlike emotions and feelings for the first time in their lives. And because these emotions are new, they are also surprising in their intensity and very unpredictable. These emotions will stabilize as the years pass, but these early emotional experiences will be very formative.

It is important therefore to give junior highers religious experiences that will allow them to "feel" God's presence and to sense his love. They need the kind of positive emotional experiences that will validate their understanding of the Christian faith. Joy, wonder, sorrow, guilt, compassion, praise, and peace—all these emotions that are an important part of the Christian faith, junior highers are now capable of internalizing. They need to feel deeply sorry for their sins and they also need to experience the joy of salvation. When junior highers shed tears, they are real tears and represent real feelings, which will have a significant impact on their lives.

Worship services ought to be emotional experiences, but in most cases, they are not. Sermons and liturgies, reciting creeds and singing hard-to-understand hymns usually carry little emotional weight for junior highers. This is why there is real value in taking kids to camps, retreats, and other places where they can worship God and receive the kind of "mountain-top experience" that may not last forever but will never be forgotten. These experiences are formative in the spiritual development of young people. We must never play on the emotions of junior highers, nor manipulate them emotionally, but we can give them opportunities to experience God's presence very deeply.

Junior highers also need to know that faith is not at all

dependent on feelings. Faith in Christ sometimes makes a person feel euphoric or peaceful or confident, but faith in Christ is *not* the result of these feelings. The emotions of junior highers fluctuate a great deal. They need the assurance that Christ is always with them, even when they are despondent, ashamed, afraid, angry, or upset. They are just as much a Christian at these times as when they are feeling great. God is constant; we change. We are the ones who are on the rollercoaster, sometimes up and sometimes down. Junior highers are going to experience a variety of feelings, some good and some bad, and they need to know that Christ is always there and understands all of them.

If junior highers seem restless, bored, distracted, or full of giggles during a worship service or when they are expected to pay attention, it is not necessarily because they are unspiritual. They are just junior highers, with a faith that is "under construction." Just as they are learning how to solve the mysteries of algebra and to handle the disappointment of a broken friendship, so they are trying to fully grasp what it means to call oneself a "Christian." As junior-high workers, we need to take their journey seriously, have patience with them, and give them every opportunity to grow and to mature as fellow members of the body of Christ.

JUNIOR HIGHERS HAVE TROUBLE LIVING THEIR FAITH

One of the most frustrating aspects of junior-high ministry is that young adolescents are not very good at connecting what they believe (or say they believe) with what they do. In other words, they don't "practice what they preach." David Elkind uses the term "apparent hypocrisy" to describe this characteristic of early adolescence. Junior highers are often very idealistic, and "talk a good game," as the expression goes, but they usually fail to carry out the actions that would seem to follow logically from their professed ideals.[5] Unfortunately, this makes them look like hypocrites—people who say one thing and do another.

But they are not being hypocritical in the same way that we would think an adult hypocritical. Ordinarily when an adult shows hypocritical behavior, we assume that he or she has the intelligence

133

required to understand fully that you should not say one thing and do something else that is obviously contradictory. But junior highers have not yet developed the ability to relate theory to practice, or faith to works. This is why a junior higher can express strong views about what is fair or honest and then, without a moment's hesitation, act in a very unfair and dishonest manner. I have listened to my thirteen-year-old son berate his little sister for taking things out of his bedroom and using them without his permission and then observed the same boy taking *my* tools off *my* workbench and using them without *my* permission. It would be unfair for me to conclude that my son is a hypocrite. It will just take some time for him to learn that there needs to be a vital and consistent relationship between what he believes and what he does.

This is one reason why junior highers sometimes "live two lives"—the one that attends church and the one that goes to school and hangs out with friends. Those two lives may be completely different from each other and very inconsistent, but the junior higher living them will not perceive that there is a problem—or at least not a serious one.

Obviously, the Christian life requires that there be a connection between faith and everyday life. It is not enough just to believe. Faith must be acted out and lived for it to have validity. But while this is true, we must not expect too much from our junior highers too soon. We must be patient with them and recognize that they are doing well just to express their values and beliefs verbally (if they do). In time, they will discover the need to back up those beliefs with their actions.

We can help junior highers learn this by giving them opportunities to be "doers of the Word." They will understand the connection between faith and works much better if they can experience it for themselves. This kind of experiential learning is sometimes called *praxis*, a term taken from the Greek word for "action." It is one of the best ways to teach junior highers. For example, if you want your junior highers to understand the scriptural idea that "we serve Christ by serving others," then do something more than have a Bible study about it. Take them somewhere where they can actually serve. Have them go and distribute food at a rescue mission, or visit people in a convalescent home, or do yard work for shut-ins. Help them to see firsthand how their beliefs translate into actions.

In the classroom, we need to emphasize the practical aspects of the Christian faith. Young adolescents are not going to be helped a great deal by studying a history of the twelve tribes of Israel. But they will be helped by discussing how the Christian faith impacts their friendships, their family life, their sexuality, their TV viewing habits, and so on.

Recently the American Lung Association tested several anti-smoking ad campaigns directed at young adolescents. The most effective one was a campaign that featured model Brooke Shields with cigarettes sticking out of her ears, and the accompanying headline "Smoking Spoils Your Looks." It was successful because it was practical. As we all know, young people have a keen interest in their looks. On the other hand, they aren't yet concerned about things like cancer and emphysema. (Those are perceived by adolescents as adult problems.)

If we want the gospel to make a difference in the lives of junior highers, we must be careful to show them how the Christian faith impacts their lives in the here and now. Junior highers need to see that the gospel has practical applications. If we can demonstrate to junior highers a few of the ways in which Christ can enrich their lives and meet their needs, they will soon realize that Christianity can be much more than a private set of beliefs and doctrines. It can change the way they live.

JUNIOR-HIGH FAITH INCLUDES FAILURE

When I was a junior higher, my biggest problem with the Christian life was not so much *not knowing what to do* as *being unable to do it*. I was taught that good Christians do not sin, or at least they don't sin very much. If they did sin, they were extremely minor sins, more like little mistakes that were forgiven instantly or hardly worth forgiving at all. But I was a sinner, sinning big sins instead of little ones, and as a result, I was constantly "losing my faith."

Many Christian junior highers experience this. They hear

again and again that the Christian life is keeping the Ten Commandments, obeying your parents, loving your neighbor, sitting quietly in church, keeping a smile on your face, acting like an adult, and so on, and they find such a life impossible to live. So they just give up.

To be sure, the church should call Christians to high standards of living, but we must be careful not to discourage our junior-high kids in the process. We need to let kids know that they can fail and still be a Christian. Almost by definition, a junior higher's life is full of failure, and junior highers need to know that Christ will be with them even in the midst of failure. God does not expect perfection from them. Their perfection, after all, has been given to them as a free gift through Jesus Christ.

In this regard, junior highers can begin to understand the meaning of commitment. Commitment has more to do with failure than it does with success. If you are committed to something, then you hang in there and keep going even when things aren't going too well. Historians claim that the inventor Thomas Edison made over nine hundred light bulbs before he finally made one that actually worked. In other words, he failed nine hundred times. Although he must have been discouraged at times, he stayed with it simply because he was committed to inventing a light bulb. He didn't give up.

The Christian life is a lot like that. You don't get it right the first time or even the second. Every time Edison made a light bulb that didn't work, he learned one more way *not* to make a light bulb. It was actually a positive experience. Maybe what we need to do is to help our junior highers learn from their mistakes, rather than be defeated by them. Let junior highers be junior highers. They are not going to act like adults. Spiritual growth takes time.

JUNIOR-HIGH FAITH IS IDEALISTIC
It is part of the early adolescent paradox that even in the midst of struggle, failure, and doubt, junior highers are extremely idealistic. They have a strong desire to be committed to something and to make their lives count. It is not uncommon for junior highers to list as career choices occupations relating to service, such as doctor, nurse, missionary, and teacher.

For this reason, it is important they be given many opportunities to serve and to use the gifts that God has given to them. Their idealism, while it may be strong during the early adolescent years, will diminish over the years if not given expression. Junior-high workers in the church should find as many ways as possible to channel the energies and enthusiasm of junior highers into positive activities that allow them to give of themselves and to see the results of their efforts. They need to feel the significance and affirmation that comes from doing things that are worthwhile and that benefit others.

Junior highers need to know that they are important and that God can use them right now. They are not the future high-school group. Neither are they the "church of tomorrow," as they are often called. I heard a seventh-grade girl once respond to that description of the youth group with this question: "Don't they know I'm alive right now?" We need to include junior highers in the church of today.

Some kids may feel that they were hopelessly short-changed when God was distributing the talents, gifts, and abilities necessary for becoming a "somebody" in God's scheme of things. A certain degree of discouragement might set in when they compare themselves with biblical or historical heroes of the faith, popular Christian celebrities of today, or adult Christians they know, such as the pastor or the youth director. Despite a genuine desire to accomplish much and to serve in some way, there is often the overriding fear that they are miserably unqualified and ill-equipped.

We can help junior highers to know that God can and will use them just the way they are. There is a story that I like to tell junior highers about a little girl who wanted to become a great pianist, but all she could play on the piano was the simple little tune "Chopsticks." No matter how hard she tried, that was the best she could do. Her parents decided after some time to arrange for a great maestro to teach her to play properly. And of course, the little girl was delighted.

When the little girl and her parents arrived at the maestro's mansion for the first lesson, she climbed up onto the piano bench in front of the maestro's grand concert piano and immediately began playing "Chopsticks." Her embarrassed parents told her to stop, but the maestro encouraged her to continue. He then took a seat on the bench next to the little girl and began to play along with her, adding chords, runs, and arpeggios. The little girl continued to play "Chopsticks." The parents couldn't believe their ears. What they heard was a beautiful piano duet, played by their daughter and the maestro, and amazingly enough the central theme of it was "Chopsticks."

Junior highers may only have "Chopsticks" to offer to God right now, but God sits on the piano bench beside them. He can take their *little* and turn it into *much*. We just need to encourage junior highers to keep on playing.

JUNIOR-HIGH FAITH NEEDS MODELS

An important factor in the spiritual development of junior highers is whether they have models of the Christian faith they can pattern themselves after. Most of what a young person learns about the gospel and about life in general is passed on not by words but by example. Therefore, it is important to surround junior highers with people they can look up to and who will inspire them to follow their example and follow Jesus Christ, the ultimate model for all of us.

The need for models is one of the reasons junior highers are such hero-worshippers. They are easily led (or misled) by anyone who is able to capture their admiration and allegiance. In many cases, this amounts to near worship of teen idols, singers, and actors who are marketed directly to this age group in the media and elsewhere. Howard and Stoumbis say this about models:

> This is the time for admiration and imitation of the hero figure, which makes it important that the proper figures for emulation are presented to the adolescent. While their parents and teachers are no longer likely to be the persons to be imitated and admired, partly because of their fallibility, familiarity, and authority symbols, the early adolescent will still seek an older model to emulate—preferably one who is competent and successful by his adolescent standards.[6]

It makes good sense to point our young people toward models who are willing to identify themselves with Jesus Christ. They don't have to be famous or talented, although I am thankful for the Christian recording artists and Christian sports figures who have become successful and accepted by the teenage crowd. We need more of those kind of people.

But even more important than "celebrity Christians," we need to surround our junior highers with adult role models who care about them. As we discussed in chapter four, early adolescents need and want adult friends who are willing to lead them across the bridge from childhood to adulthood. Rather than isolate our young people from the adults in the church by creating a "youth ghetto," we need to find ways to encourage interaction between the young and the old. I encourage and pray for all the men in my church because I recognize that they are role models for my thirteen-year-old son. Recently while I was out of town on a trip, a good friend of mine invited Nathan to go with him on a ski trip for the weekend. I was delighted, not just because it provided a weekend activity for my son, but because it provided an opportunity for him to spend some time with a good man who cared about him and who was modeling the Christian faith in front of him.

Like it or not, we who work with junior highers are more often than not thrust into the position of model, simply because we are one of the few adults who have regular contact with the kids. They watch us, and we show them what adult Christians are like. We should not be intimidated by this; we do not have to be perfect and give kids the wrong impression. That's why it's a good idea to let kids see you in different settings, not just at church in a suit and tie. They need to see you at home, with your family, on the job, and when your hair is all messed up.

On the other hand, we should realize that this is a great responsibility. We should strive to set as good an example for our junior highers as we can. We cannot let our lives contradict the gospel that we represent.

Most importantly, we need to love our junior highers. They will follow us and be discipled not because of what we teach or say, but because of our love for them. The renowned psychologist Bruno Bettelheim recently made this observation about Christ's ministry to his disciples:

Most of us when hearing or using the word *disciple* are likely to be reminded of the biblical apostles. Their deepest wish was to emulate Christ. They made him their guide not just because they believed in his teachings but because of their love for him and his love for them. Without such mutual love the Master's teaching and example, convincing though they were, would never have persuaded the disciples to change their lives and beliefs as radically as they did.[7]

Part III

PROGRAMING

9.
PROGRAMING FOR JUNIOR HIGH GROUPS

What does a successful junior-high program look like? How many meetings per week should there be? How many adults should be involved? Should junior highers and senior highers meet together or separately? Which curriculum is best? Are today's kids too sophisticated to play games? What about confirmation classes? How do I get my junior highers excited about Bible study? Should junior highers participate in service projects? How do I motivate them to come? And, what is the meaning of the universe?

Tough questions, all of them. Unfortunately, there are no easy answers that will hold true for everyone in all situations. A good answer here might be a bad answer there. It's like telling someone, "Water is good." That statement is true if you are thirsty, but not if you are drowning. In the same way, it's very difficult to be specific about programing for junior-high groups. What works for one group may not work at all for another. People often ask me, "What should my junior-high program look like?" My best answer is usually something like this: "Do whatever it takes to meet the needs of your kids." That could mean lots of meetings or no meetings at all, lots of activities or none at all. Lest this sound like a complete evasion of the question, let me remind you that junior-high ministry is first of all relational. The key is *people*, not *programs*. If you love junior highers and are able to relate to them well, just about any program will probably work.

THE SUCCESSFUL JUNIOR-HIGH PROGRAM

There are a few things, however, that can be said about successful junior-high programs which will be true most of the time. As I stated in chapter three, programs for junior highers need to be designed around an informed understanding of the needs of early adolescents. We cannot make the mistake of "drawing targets around our arrows." Using what we know to be true about junior highers as a guide, we can create programs that will not only work, but will help our junior highers to learn and to grow in a healthy and wholesome environment.

Joan Lipsitz and Gayle Dorman of the Center for Early Adolescence have identified seven key characteristics that are common to successful programs and respond well to the developmental needs of this age group.[1] These characteristics are grounded solidly in current adolescent research, and I believe that they can be very helpful in both planning and evaluating junior-high programs in the church. I will list them here and explain each one briefly. I will also add a couple of characteristics of my own.

1. **Diversity.** Because junior highers are growing and changing very rapidly, and at a variety of rates, an appropriate activity for one young person might be completely inappropriate for another. Therefore, when programing for *groups* of junior highers, it is best to provide a wide variety of experiences and activities. This could mean providing different kinds of programs from one week to the next, or perhaps a variety of choices or "electives" each week. Remember that it is possible to have two junior highers in the same group who are light years apart developmentally. Take that into consideration and provide more than one way for kids to learn and to be involved.

For example, if you are doing a study about the concept of "Christian love," try approaching it from a number of different angles. You might have a "Bible Word Search," which appeals to those who enjoy that sort of thing and an essay-writing exercise for those who are capable of thinking about the subject on a deeper level. You could allow some of the group to create a collage or a mural that describes Christian love, while others brainstorm a list of "things to do" that would demonstrate Christian love in the family. Provide enough variety that everyone has an opportunity to learn and to enjoy the experience equally.

2. **Self-Exploration and Definition.** Rapidly changing bodies and minds require new ways of thinking, new experiences, and new reactions from others. Junior highers need opportunities to get a new window on life as they move from childhood into adulthood, and they need time to reflect on how they fit into their new world. They need adventure—field trips, service projects, environments and experiences they have never had before—and time to discover for themselves who they are and the kind of person they want to be.

This is one reason why the junior-high years are the perfect time to get kids out of the classroom and into the real world as often as possible. The idea "Tour of Your Life" (page 203) is a good example of this. I know a youth worker who takes his youth group to an incredible assortment of places around town for their regular weekly meetings, and the kids love it. For example, one week the group meets at a local securities firm, and there they discuss the topic of money. Another week, they meet inside the county jail, and there they discuss the topic of law. The next week, the group might visit a local slum, and there discuss the subject of Christ's concern for the poor. Experiences like this leave an indelible imprint on the lives of junior highers.

3. **Meaningful Participation.** As junior highers develop more mature social, physical, and intellectual skills, they need opportunities to use them. There is a tremendous amount of untapped potential waiting for youth workers who will take the time to adapt responsibilities and tasks to match the skills and abilities of junior highers. They must not be given more responsibility than they can handle (so as not to frustrate them), but they do need to feel that they have a contribution to make that is important and appreciated. Junior highers need to be involved—active participants rather than passive spectators. This, incidentally, is one way to eliminate the "discipline problem" that is common in many junior-high groups. Kids who are involved are much less likely to become discipline problems.

Recently, a junior-high worker who was taking a group of kids on a long bus trip came up with a great idea that illustrates this point. He assigned everyone on the bus a job. His list of jobs was titled "In-Transit Occupation Opportunities" and included such positions as "Sound Technician" (operates the tape deck), "Navigator" (tracks progress on map), "Interior Recreation Assistant" (helps with games), "Secretary" (writes down everything that happens on the bus), and "Bus Attendant #1" (checks oil, tires, lights, and so on at each stop). The result was not only a much better behaved group of kids on the bus, but a lot less work for the driver and adult leaders.

4. **Positive Interaction with Peers and Adults.** The two most significant influences on early adolescents are peers and adult figures outside the family. Parents have been the most important influence in their childhood and will continue to be important, but now the junior higher seeks support, affirmation, and criticism from trusted friends and adults. A successful youth program will take advantage of this new focus and will foster a sense of community and belonging among the kids and provide adults who will take time to build relationships with each young person.

This is one reason why I believe that effective junior-high ministry is easier in smaller groups. It is difficult to build relationships and community in a group that is so large that some kids are missed. If your junior-high group is large, then it would be wise to break it down into smaller units that have identities of their own. One method that I have used is to break the group down into "teams" with "coaches" (adult sponsors) who work exclusively with their small group of kids. Of course, there are times when the entire group needs to be together, but most of the time, in classes and in discussion, the smaller group works best.

"Positive interaction" can take many forms. For example, whenever a group is playing together, talking to each other, working together, serving together, and so on, positive interaction is likely to take place. It is important to understand, however, that certain kinds of things foster good interaction and community, and other things prevent it. For example, meetings and activities in which the kids are mere spectators do not allow for much positive interaction. Too often, the church is like a football game: 22,000 people badly in need of exercise up in the bleachers watching 22 people badly in need of rest down on the field.

5. **Physical Activity.** Junior highers are well known for their bursts of energy as well as their periods of laziness. They need plenty of opportunities to stretch, wiggle, and exercise their rapidly growing bodies. This is one reason their attention span is relatively short. I recommend that activities be divided into short segments that provide a change of pace every ten to fifteen minutes. The timely insertion of a game, an audio visual, a walk, a discussion, or a rest period will do wonders to keep kids interested and involved. Competitive games that include physical activity are very popular with junior highers, so long as they take into consideration the diversity in size, coordination, and athletic skill of the age group.

6. **Competence and Achievement.** Junior highers have an overwhelming desire to do something well and to receive admiration for what they have done. They hunger for chances to prove themselves, especially in ways that receive praise from others if they succeed and won't be too devastated if they fail. They are often afraid to take great risks, but when there is a good chance for success and when help is provided, they are anxious to try. Youth workers can greatly increase their junior highers' sense of self-esteem and self-confidence by providing opportunities from an activity as simple as successfully participating in a game, or an achievement as difficult as playing a musical instrument in front of a large group. Junior highers can do service projects, participate in a worship service, help plan a Vacation Bible School, or teach a Sunday school class with good results.

7. **Structure and Clear Limits.** Young adolescents are keenly aware that they live in a society governed by rules, and they want to understand their limits within that system. They want freedom, but they also want to know the boundaries of that freedom. They need to be given well-defined rules and limits, but unlike younger children, they are capable of helping to formulate those rules and limits, and they require that they be fair and equitable. If discipline is an ongoing problem in your youth group, then it could be that the rules are not clear, or that the young people have been deprived of a significant role in the formation and discussion of the rules that they are expected to live by.

8. **Fun.** I have added this characteristic to Lipsitz and

147

Dorman's list because young adolescents, like other human beings, enjoy participating in activities and programs that are fun. But this doesn't mean programs have to be silly or shallow. Even serious times can be fun when they are done with friends and adults who are fun to be around, or when the program includes a touch of creativity. I know one group of junior highers, for example, who meet for a Bible study in a tree house. For them, Bible study is indeed fun.

Fun doesn't necessarily mean *funny*. Some people think that to make something fun, you have to have everyone rolling in the aisles with laughter. That is not true at all. Fun is simply the opposite of dull and boring. Junior highers are famous for calling everything "Boooorring!" And usually they are not being overly critical; they are just being honest. Too often, we get into a real rut with our programing and resort to the same old things again and again. Someone once said that a rut is nothing more than "a grave with both ends kicked out," and that is definitely true in junior-high ministry. If you want to make your junior-high group "fun," just try something new once in a while. Your kids will love it.

9. **Family-oriented.** I have added this characteristic as well because I believe that effective junior-high programs must take into consideration each young person's family. Parents in particular need to be included and ministered to. Just as junior highers are making a transition in life, so are their parents. They often don't understand what is happening to their child. Junior-high workers are in a very strategic position of both privilege and responsibility. We can help parents tremendously, and in so doing, we are also helping our junior highers. We need to communicate with parents, get them involved, and enlist their support.

Many youth workers have organized "Parent Support Groups" in their churches with great success. Others have published newsletters for parents to keep them informed. I have conducted seminars for parents of junior highers (and preadolescents) to inform them and to answer their questions about the changes that are (or will be) taking place in their child. Most parents are very apprehensive and afraid at this time in their lives due to all the "horror stories" that they have heard about teenagers.

We can help them tremendously and give them the encouragement they need. In return, they will do the same for us.

You should be able to select or to design effective programs that will work for your junior-high group by evaluating them in light of these nine characteristics. While no two junior-high programs should be the same, they should possess most of these characteristics in common. Almost any program, activity, or curriculum will bring positive results if these features are present. There are dozens of places to go for ideas, and numerous models worth copying, but only you can determine what will be best for your particular junior-high group.

CAMPUS MINISTRY

One of the most effective ways to build a junior-high youth group and to reach unchurched junior highers for Christ is to have an ongoing ministry on local junior-high campuses in your area. This is what is known as "campus ministry." Too often, we think of junior-high ministry as something we do strictly within the boundaries of the church. Campus ministry gets us out of the church and into the junior-high schools, which is where the kids are.

You don't have to conduct youth group meetings or Bible studies at the school to have a campus ministry. Usually all you have to do is to volunteer for something. Few people volunteer to work on a junior-high campus, so the need is great. Most junior-high schools appreciate volunteers who will serve as lunch monitors, cafeteria workers, chaperons for dances and field trips, coaches, and a variety of other positions. As a volunteer, this gives you visibility with the kids and allows you to establish positive relationships with them and with the school authorities.

A friend of mine who is the minister to junior highers at a large church in San Diego discovered a few years ago that there was a need at one junior-high school for someone to teach the Student Government class. The class is an elective for all of the student body officers, and regular teachers don't want to teach it because they don't get paid for it. So, this junior-high minister, who is qualified to teach in the public schools, volunteered to teach the class without being paid and was allowed to do so. As a result, his junior-high group at church has experienced tremendous growth, largely due to the contacts made on campus with all the student leaders.

I know one youth worker who volunteered to be the school photographer and to take pictures for the school yearbook. This gave him complete access to every single activity at the school. Another junior-high worker in our area recently volunteered to do a seminar on drug and alcohol abuse for the students at one junior-high school, and this resulted in his being invited to do the same seminar at several other schools in the area as well.

There are lots of different possibilities for campus ministry if you are willing to put forth the effort and the time. Sometimes the best thing to do is to visit the principal or the school administrator and say, "How can I help out? I'd like to serve." Don't hide the fact that you are a minister (if you are), but don't give the impression that you are only interested in making contacts for your youth group. If you do, you will more than likely be turned down. In most states there are laws that forbid religious groups from coming on campus and doing any kind of proselytising of the students. You need to respect that and not abuse your privilege. Your posture should be that of a servant. Most schools welcome people who genuinely enjoy being around junior highers, know how to relate to them, and have something positive to offer to the school. Go on campus as a *giver*, not a *getter*. Your ministry will be much more effective if you do.

10.
FUN AND GAMES FOR JUNIOR-HIGH GROUPS

It really goes without saying that junior highers have lots of energy and enjoy playing games—the more active, the better. Good games are not only fun, they are also healthy and give kids a chance to use their physical and mental skills and to relate to others in a community-building atmosphere. It is always good to include a regular time for recreation in the junior-high program of the church whenever possible. A Saturday or Sunday afternoon of games in the park or a Friday evening "Fun and Games Night" in a gym or in the church fellowship hall will nearly always be one of the most popular activities with the kids.

The most important thing, of course, is to choose the right games. While there will always be a few favorites that the kids enjoy more than others, it is best to provide a variety of games— different games that offer new challenges and new ways to have fun. Games should be playable by anyone, regardless of ability, and the competition involved should make games exciting, without becoming an end in itself. Winning should be almost irrelevant or anticlimactic to a good game. The important thing is that everyone has a good time playing the game.

For additional games, I recommend a book that I coauthored with Mike Yaconelli, *Play It!* (Zondervan, 1986). It is an up-to-date encyclopedia of games, most of which can be used successfully with junior highers. Most of the game suggestions here come from that book and are especially good with junior-high groups.

AMERICAN EAGLE

This is not a coed game. All guys or all girls line up on a line. They choose one who stands thirty feet or so away in the middle of a field. When the whistle is blown, players start running toward the guy in the middle of the field. That person tackles one (or more if he can), holds him down, and says "American Eagle" three times. Now the rest of the players are on the other side of the field and must run through two guys to get back to the original side again. The game continues until everybody has been tackled and is in the middle of the field. Give a prize to the last runner.

AMOEBA

Divide into teams and tie a sturdy rope around the team at their waists. To do this, have the team bunch up together as closely as they can and hold their hands up in the air while you tie the rope around them. After they are tied, they can race to a goal and back. Unless they work together as a team, they will go nowhere. This is a fun game for camps and outdoor activities. With small teams, this game can also be done with a hula hoop instead of a rope.

BALLOON BASKETBALL

For this game, there should be an equal number of people on the two teams. There can be any number of players on a team, but the teams must be equal. Arrange your chairs in rows (see the following diagram). One team faces in one direction; the second team faces the other direction. The two single rows of chairs on each end should face inward.

After all the players are seated, toss a balloon into the center. Using only their hands and not standing, players try to bat the balloon to the end zone they are facing. As soon as the balloon drops into the end zone over the heads of the last row of people, the team facing in that direction wins two points. If the balloon goes out of bounds, just throw it back into the center. Continue the game until one team reaches twenty points or after fifteen minutes of play.

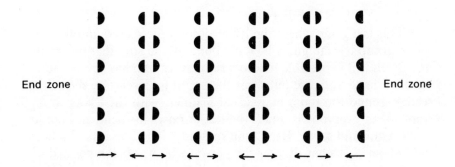

End zone

End zone

BALLOON STOMP

Everyone receives a balloon and a piece of string. Each person blows up the balloon and ties it to his ankle with the string. When the game begins, kids try to stomp and pop everyone else's balloons while keeping theirs intact.

BARNYARD

Give each person a folded piece of paper with the name of an animal written on it. The person is not to say a word or look at the paper. He is to sit down and await further instructions. (To insure equal teams, assign the same animal to every sixth person.) After everyone is seated, the group is told to look at their team name, and when the lights are turned out, they are to stand immediately and make the sound of their animals, such as these:

1. Pig
2. Horse
3. Cow
4. Chicken
5. Duck
6. Dog

As soon as they find someone else who is making the same noise, they lock arms and try to find more of their teammates. When the lights come back on, everyone sits down. The team most *together* wins. For added fun, give one guy in the crowd the word "donkey" on his paper. He'll wander around looking for more donkeys without any luck at all.

BANG, YOU'RE DEAD

This is a game where the leader knows the secret, and the rest of the group tries to guess how it's done. Make sure that the group understands it is possible to know right away who has been "shot," but they have to figure out what the secret is. Everyone should be seated around the room in a casual manner, with the leader at the front. After everyone is quiet, the leader raises his hand and points it like a gun and says, "Bang, you're dead." Then he asks, "Whom did I shoot?" It's hardly ever the person who was being pointed at. Several people will guess, and they will most likely be wrong. Then the leader announces who it was. The leader continues to shoot people but changes what he does each time.

And just what is the secret? The person who was actually shot is the first person to speak after the leader says, "Bang, you're dead." Sooner or later, someone will catch on or perhaps the leader will make it a little more obvious, which only baffles the rest of the group even more. It's fun as well as frustrating.

BIRDIE ON THE PERCH

Have players pair off and get into two concentric circles. The boys should be in the outside circle, and the girls should be in the inside circle.

At the whistle, the boys' circle begins moving clockwise and the girls' circle moves counterclockwise. When the leader yells, "Birdie on the perch!" the boys stop where they are and get down on all fours. Each girl must quickly locate her partner and sit on his back, like a horse. The last couple to get into this position is eliminated. The game continues until only one couple remains.

BUCKET BRIGADE

For this game, you need two teams. Each team lines up single file with a bucket of water on one end and an empty bucket on the other. Each team member has a paper cup. The object of the game is to transfer the water from one bucket to the other by pouring the water from cup to cup down the line. The first team to get all of the water to an empty bucket is the winner.

BEDLAM

This game requires four teams of equal size. Each team takes one corner of the room or playing field. The play area can be either square or rectangular. On a signal (whistle), each team attempts to move as quickly as possible to the corner directly across from them (diagonally) and performs an announced activity as they go. The first team to get all its members into its new corner wins that particular round. The first round can be simply running to the opposite corner, but after that you can use any number of possibilities, such as walking backward, wheelbarrow racing (one person as the wheelbarrow), a piggyback, rolling somersaults, hopping on one foot, skipping, or crab walking. There will be mass bedlam in the center as all four teams crisscross.

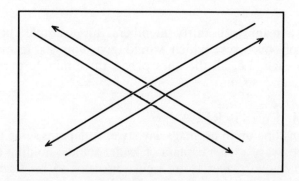

BROOM HOCKEY

This game may be played with as many as thirty or as few as five per team, but only five or six are actually on the field at one time from each team. Two teams compete by running onto the field (at the whistle), grabbing their brooms, and swatting a volleyball, placed in the center, through the opposite goal. Each team has a goalie, as in ice hockey or soccer, who can grab the ball with his hands and throw it back onto the playing field. If the ball goes out of bounds, the referee throws it back in. The ball may not be touched with hands or feet, only with a broom. Score one point for each time the ball passes between goal markers.

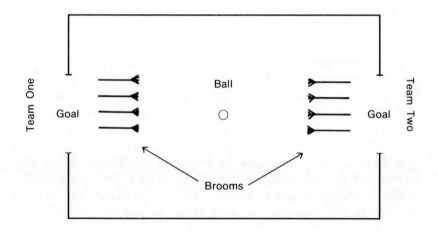

For a team with thirty members, for example, have them number off by sixes, which would give you six teams of five members each. Let all the ones play a three-minute period, then the twos, and so on.

BROOM TWIST RELAY

Teams line up in normal relay style. At a point some twenty or thirty feet away, a team captain or leader stands, holding a broom. At a signal, one player from each team runs to his team leader, takes the broom, holds it against his chest with the bristles up in the air over his head. Looking up at the broom, the player must turn around as fast as possible ten times, while the leader counts the number of turns. Then the player hands the broom back to the leader, runs back to the team, and tags the next player. Players become very dizzy, and the results are hilarious.

CINDERELLA

Arrange chairs in a circle. All the Cinderellas (girls) in the group select a chair. The Prince Charmings (guys) each pick a Cinderella and kneel in front of her. He removes her shoes and holds them in his hand. The leader calls for the shoes, and they are thrown to the middle of the circle. Then the Cinderellas blindfold their Prince Charmings. After each prince is blindfolded, the leader rearranges and mixes the shoes in the middle.

At a signal, all the Prince Charmings crawl to the circle and attempt to find their Cinderellas' shoes. The Cinderellas can only help verbally, shouting instructions to their men. After finding the shoes, the princes crawl back to their girls (again guided by verbal instructions). They place the shoes (right one on right foot, left one on left foot) on the girls and then remove their blindfolds. The game continues until the last contestant succeeds.

CLUMPS
This game can be used for as many as one thousand. People crowd to the center with their arms at their sides. They are instructed to keep moving and crowding toward the center. The leader blows a whistle or foghorn to stop all movement and immediately shouts a number. If the number is four, for instance, everyone must get into groups of four, lock arms, and sit down. Referees then eliminate all those not in groups of four. This is repeated, with different numbers each time, until all have been eliminated.

A variation of this game is called "Tin Pan Bang Bang." In this game, no number is shouted. Instead, the leader bangs on a stainless steel pot with a big metal spoon. The players must listen and count the number of bangs. If the leader stops banging on the pot after five bangs, then the players must get into groups of five.

You can add a further element to the game by dividing the group into two separate teams. Then, the players mingle around until the leader shouts (or bangs out) a number. At that point, they must get into a group of the designated number but only with members of their own team.

THE COORDINATION CLAP
This is a crowd breaker that you can use anytime, as many times as you want. It is always fun, gets good laughs, and involves everyone. The procedure is very simple. You move one hand up and one hand down (vertically), and the group must clap every time your hands cross in the middle. If your hands stop before

crossing, then the audience must not clap. When you fake the group out by stopping just before your hands cross, the fun begins. Go fast, then slow, and point out people who goof it up. When anyone goofs, he is out of the game. Award whoever remains a prize.

DOMINO

This is a great game for larger groups that is not only fun to play, but fun to watch as well. It's also easy to play and requires no props. Teams line up in single-file lines parallel to each other. There should be the same number of people (exactly) in each line, and everyone should face toward the front of the line. At a signal (whistle), the first person in each line squats, then each person in turn squats, all the way down to the end of the team's line. (You cannot squat down until the person immediately in front of you squats first.) The last person in line squats and then quickly stands up again, and in reverse, each person stands up in succession. (Again, you cannot stand up until the person behind you first stands up.) The first team with the person standing at the front of the line is the winner.

This game looks much like standing dominoes, where each domino falls in succession, except here the dominoes first go down, then back up again. It works best with at least twenty-five or so in each line (the more the better). Have the group try it several times for speed.

THE FORTY-INCH DASH

This is a quick little game that is fun to play and to watch. Give three or more kids a forty-inch piece of string with a marshmallow tied to one end. At a signal, each person puts the loose end in his mouth and, without using his hands, "eats" his way to the marshmallow. The first person to reach the marshmallow is the winner.

FOUR TEAM DODGEBALL

This is a fast-moving game that is best played in a gym or similar room. Divide the group into four teams of equal size. If you have a basketball court marked on the floor, this can be used as the playing area; otherwise, you will need to mark off your own boundaries with tape or by some other method. The floor is divided into quadrants similar to the diagram below.

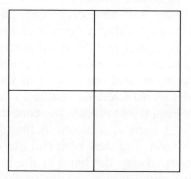

Each team is assigned one of the four areas, and members cannot leave their assigned area during the game. A volleyball, beach ball, or playground ball should be used (nothing as hard as a basketball). The rules are basically the same as regular dodgeball, except that a player may throw the ball at anyone in any of the other three quadrants. If a player is hit below the belt with the ball, he is out of the game. If the ball misses and goes out-of-bounds, the referee tosses the ball in to the team occupying the square the ball went out-of-bounds from. If a player catches the ball before it hits the floor, without dropping it, the player who threw it is out. The winning team is the team that still has at least one player after the other teams have been eliminated or the team with the most players left at the end of a specified time limit.

HAT AND GO SEEK

Here's a game that combines the best of tag and hide-and-go-seek. One person wears an old hat, hides his eyes, and gives the rest of the group one minute to run and hide. Then, the hat-wearer begins to search. (The hat must be worn, not carried.)

When someone is found and tagged, that person must wear the

hat, cover his eyes for twenty counts, and continue the search. Each person should keep track of how many times he wears the hat. The one who wears it the least number of times wins.

HUMAN SCAVENGER HUNT

Divide into teams and have each team choose a leader. All team members must stay within a designated area. A judge stands in a position that is equidistant from all teams. For example, if there are four teams, then the teams can position themselves in the four corners of the room and the judge can stand in the middle.

The judge calls a characteristic similar to the ones below, and the leader on each team tries to locate someone on the team that fits the characteristic. As soon as someone is found, the leader grabs that person by the hand, and they both run like crazy to the judge. The first team leader to slap the hand of the judge (pulling along the proper person) wins points for the team.

Here are some sample characteristics: Someone who . . .
1. Has blue eyes and brown hair.
2. Received all A's on his last report card.
3. Ate at McDonald's today.
4. Jogs daily.
5. Is going steady.
6. Likes broccoli.
7. Sent a friend a card today.
8. Memorized a Bible verse this week.

HUSTLE

For this game, everyone has to really *hustle*. You need something that everyone can scramble through or under (under a bench, through a drain pipe or large cardboard box or old car, under a table). One team at a time lines up single file on one side of the bench (as an example), and at "Go!" each person hustles under the bench and gets back in line as quickly as possible. Each team has an impartial counter who counts the kids as they pass under the bench. The object is to see how many kids (one-at-a-time) can hustle under the bench in one minute (or some other time limit). Each team gets a try, and then the game begins.

INDOOR MURDERBALL

For this game, you need a room that is nearly indestructible, with plenty of room to run. Two teams of equal size line up on opposite walls, about three feet from the wall. Team members then number off.

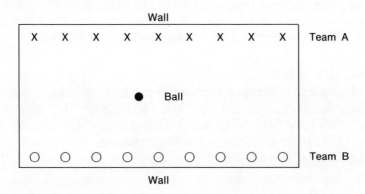

A ball is placed in the middle of the room. (Any large ball will work.) The leader calls a number, and the two players with that number (one from each team) run to the middle and try to hit the opposing team's wall with the ball. The team standing in front of the wall tries to stop the ball.

Players attempt to get the ball to its goal any way they can—carrying it across, throwing, kicking, rolling, whatever. Anything is legal.

INNER-TUBE RELAY

Each team divides into couples. The couples should be of the same sex, rather than boy-girl couples. Each team then lines up in different corners of the room, if possible. Inner tubes (one for each team) are placed in the center of the room. Each couple must run to the inner tube and squeeze through the tube together, starting with the tube over their heads and working it down. The first team to have all their couples finish the relay wins.

161

JAWBREAKER CROWDBREAKER

Here's a crazy way to get kids divided into groups for either a learning activity or game. Give each person a jawbreaker (candy) to suck on during the first few minutes of the meeting or event. Make sure that you distribute several different colors, with an equal number of each. After the kids have enjoyed the candy for a while, tell them to stick out their tongues and to find others who have the same color tongue as they do. The first group or team to locate all its members (with the same color tongues) is the winner.

KING OF THE CIRCLE

This game is always a winner, especially with boys. It is a very physical game. Simply draw a circle on the floor (or a square for KING OF THE SQUARE) and have everyone get inside. Then at "Go," the object is to throw everyone else out of the circle while trying to stay in yourself.

LONGJOHN STUFF

This is a hilarious game that is always fun with any group. You will need to get two pairs of long underwear and about one hundred small (six inch round) balloons. You will also need a straight pin. Divide into two teams. Each team selects one person from their team to put on a pair of longjohns. It would be best for them to pick someone who is not too big. The longjohns should just go over the kid's regular clothes. Each team should also select two or three balloon stuffers.

When the kids are ready, throw out an equal number of balloons to the two teams. The team members must blow them up (all the way), tie them, and pass them to the stuffers who try to stuff all of them into the longjohns. The object is to see which team can stuff the most balloons into their person's longjohns within the given time limit. Usually, about two minutes is long enough. After both contestants have been sufficiently stuffed, stop the two teams and have the two people in the longjohns stand still. (Now would be a good time for some pictures.)

To count the balloons, begin with the one who appears to have the fewest balloons and pop them with a pin (through the longjohns), while the team counts. (Be careful you don't stick the contestant with the pin.)

MAD LIBS

This game is a great crowdbreaker for any age group and is available in book form from most book and stationery stores. It is a collection of stories with certain key words, such as nouns, adjectives, and persons, left out. The audience supplies the words as they are asked for by the leader, without knowing anything about the story. The words the audience supplies should be as ridiculous as possible, and the leader writes them into the story as provided in *Mad Libs*. The results are always entertaining. The books are distributed by Pocket Books, Inc., 630 Fifth Ave., New York, and there are many editions of the game, such as *Mad Libs, Son of Mad Libs, Scooper Mad Libs*.

MUSICAL HATS

Pick six or more junior highers to stand in a circle, each facing the back of another person. In other words, they would all be looking clockwise, or all counterclockwise. Five of the kids put on hats (or you can use paper paint buckets) and when the music starts (or at a signal), each kid grabs the hat on the person's head in front of him and puts it on his own head. That way, the hats are moving around the circle from head to head until the music stops (or the next signal). Whoever is left without a hat is out of the game. Remove one hat and continue until there are only two kids left. They stand back-to-back, grabbing the hat off each other's head, and when the music stops, the one wearing the hat is the winner.

POOP DECK

Here's a great game for ten to one hundred. Play in a fairly large room or outside. Clearly mark off three sections on the floor with tape or chalk. One section is the Poop Deck, one the Main Deck, and the last the Quarter Deck. Begin with everyone standing on the Poop Deck. Call the name of a deck (even the one that they are standing in), and the kids then run to the deck that you have called. The last person on the deck is out. If the kids are on Poop

Deck, for example, and you call, "Poop Deck," any kid who crosses the line, jumps the gun, or in any other away (except being pushed) goes off the Poop Deck section is out. The game continues until one person is the winner.

POOPDECK	MAINDECK	QUARTERDECK

Other hints on playing this game: Give the kids a few trial runs to warm up and to get the hang of the game; call the decks loudly and distinctly; and occasionally point to the opposite deck you call to confuse them thoroughly.

MUSICAL SQUIRT GUN

This exciting game can be played with a group ranging from six to thirty, indoors or outdoors. Have the group sit in a circle either on chairs or on the floor. A loaded squirt gun is passed around the circle until the music stops or until the leader says, "Stop." The person who is holding the squirt gun at that time must leave the game. But before he leaves, he may squirt the person on his left twice or on his right twice or once each. After his chair is removed, the circle moves in, and the game continues. The last person left is declared the winner.

The gun must be passed with two hands and received with two hands. (Otherwise it will be frequently dropped and break.) It is best to have a second loaded squirt gun on hand to be substituted for the empty one. An assistant can refill the original gun while the second one is being used. Be sure to emphasize that only two squirts are allowed, or you will be continually refilling the squirt guns.

SARDINES

This game is actually hide-and-seek in reverse. The group chooses one person to be IT. This person hides while the rest of the group counts to one hundred (or a signal is given). Now the group sets out to find the hidden person. Each person should look individually, but small groups (two or three) may look together. When a person finds IT, he hides with IT instead of telling the rest of the group. The hiding place may be changed an unlimited number of times during any game. The last person to find the hidden group, which has now come to resemble a group of sardines, is the loser or IT for the next game.

SHUFFLE YOUR BUNS

Here's a wild game you can play over and over again. Arrange chairs in a circle, so everyone has a chair. There should be two extra chairs in the circle. Each person sits in a chair, except for two people in the middle who try to sit in the two vacant chairs. The persons sitting in the chairs keep moving around from chair to chair to prevent the two in the middle from sitting down. If one or both of the two in the middle manage to sit in a chair, the person on their right replaces them in the middle of the circle and then tries to sit in an empty chair.

SUPER SACK RELAY

Divide into teams with ten people on each team. Have a brown paper bag for each team with the following items in each:
Jar of baby food
Green onion
Can of cola (warm)
Raw carrot
Piece of cream cheese (wrapped in wax paper)
Box of Cracker Jacks
Peanut butter sandwich
An orange
An apple
A banana
At a signal, the first member of each team runs to the bag and

must eat the first item he pulls out. Sponsors should make sure items are satisfactorily finished before the person goes back and tags the next member of the team. First team to eat everything in the sack wins.

STEAL THE BACON

This is an old favorite, which most groups love to play. Divide into two teams and line up the teams facing each other behind two lines (twenty to thirty feet apart). Each team should number off, so they have the same numbered players, but in opposite directions (see diagram). A handkerchief or towel is placed in the center, at a point equidistant from both teams.

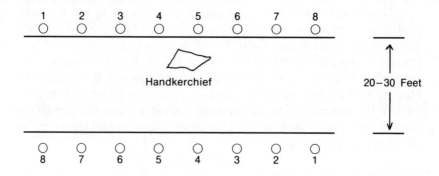

The leader calls a number. The player on each team having that number runs to the center and tries to snatch the handkerchief and return to his goal without being tagged by the other player. The more skilled players will run into the center and hover over the handkerchief until he can snatch it and run when his opponent is off guard. Each successful return gains one point for the team. After each successful tag or score, the handkerchief is returned to the center, and another number is called. Play for a designated number of points. The leader should call numbers in a way that builds suspense. All numbers should be included, but it is well to repeat a number now and then to keep all players alert. Also, maintain interest by calling two or more numbers simultaneously (involving four or more players).

STICKER MIXER

Here's a good get-acquainted activity for large groups. Write everyone's name on a sticker (pressure-sensitive round ones work best) and distribute them at random. Have everyone stick the label somewhere on his face. Then, each player tries to find his own name on someone else's face and sticks it on his own shirt. These two players stick together until the unstickered player finds his name. This is a good way for kids to see a lot of faces in a short time.

TECHNICOLOR STOMP

Here's a good indoor game, which is really wild. You will need lots of colored balloons. Divide into teams and assign each team a color (red, blue, orange, yellow). Then give each team an equal number of balloons of their color. For example, the red team would be given a certain number (like twenty) red balloons. They begin by blowing up all the balloons and tying them. When the actual game begins, the balloons from all the teams are released onto the floor, and the object is to stomp on and pop all the balloons of the other teams while attempting to protect your own team's balloons. After the time is up (two or three minutes probably), the popping of balloons stops, and each team gathers up its remaining balloons. The team with the most balloons left is the winner.

TETHERBALL JUMP

Here's an old game that groups really enjoy. Have ten to twenty players form a circle. You get in the center of the circle with a tetherball (a ball attached to a rope about eight feet long). Take the rope in your hand and begin making circles with the ball, about six inches off the ground. The circle of players then moves in closer, and each person must jump over the ball. You keep the ball going around and around, getting faster and faster until someone goofs and is out. Whoever remains in the circle is the winner. As the game progresses, you may make the ball go faster and/or higher. Two leaders (ball twirlers) are recommended to take shifts in the center in case of dizziness.

TRUE-FALSE SCRAMBLE

Here's an active game that can also be educational. You will need to compile a list of questions that can be answered "true" or "false." These can be Bible questions or general knowledge questions.

Divide your players into two teams seated across from each other in two rows (see diagram). At one end is an empty chair marked "true," and at the other end an empty chair marked "false." Players on each team should number off, so there are the same numbers on each team.

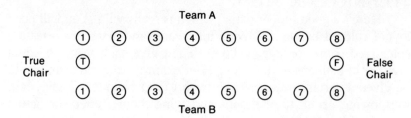

To play the game, the leader reads a question and then calls a number. The two players with that number (one from each team) jump up and try to sit in the chair that represents the correct answer to the question. The first to sit wins a point for his team. It's a wild game, especially if you throw in a few hard questions.

WADDLE WALK RELAY

This one requires some real coordination, but anyone can do it. Players must walk to a goal and back with a balloon held between their knees and a cup of water balanced on their heads. If either the balloon breaks (or drops) or the cup of water falls off, the player must start over.

11.
SPECIAL EVENTS FOR
JUNIOR-HIGH GROUPS

Junior highers have a lot more free time on their hands than most older teens, so it's a good idea to program accordingly. Unlike high schoolers, they don't drive, have weekend jobs, date, or have school football and basketball games to go to. They often just stay home and complain about having "nuthin' to do."

Taking advantage of this, many junior-high groups plan at least one special event each weekend—on a Friday or Saturday night, during the day on Saturday, or maybe on a Sunday afternoon. Other groups limit their social activities to only one per month or maybe twice monthly. Regardless of their frequency, junior highers really enjoy getting together with their friends just for fun, and they love to get away from home whenever they can. Socials and special events can and should be an integral part of any well-planned junior-high program.

There are many possibilities for a special event: a party at someone's home, a trip to an amusement park or to the beach, going bowling, skating, or miniature golfing, or attending a good movie or concert. You can do overnighters (a "Lock In" in which kids sleep (?) overnight at the church in their sleeping bags). There are dozens of unusual and fun activities that you can create yourself similar to the ones suggested here. There is an infinite number of possibilities, most of which are effective ways to provide quick relief from the usual routine of youth-group programing, as well as provide good opportunities for outreach and evangelism. Kids will often bring their friends to a special event when they won't even think about bringing their friends to a church meeting. The other obvious benefit of special events is fellowship and community building. Kids need plenty of opportunities to enjoy being together socially, and special events are ideal for that.

The ideas listed here are especially good for junior-high groups. Most of them come from another book, which I have coauthored with Mike Yaconelli, called *Creative Socials and Special Events* (Zondervan, 1986). There are lots more ideas in that book that can be used successfully with junior highers.

A.B.C. SCAVENGER HUNT

Here's one that is easy and adds the element of chance to an ordinary scavenger hunt. Rather than creating a list of scavenger hunt items ahead of time, prepare several slips of paper with a letter of the alphabet written on each one. It's best if the letters are frequently-used consonants, such as "T," "C," "R," and the like. There should be one letter per team.

Each team draws one letter from a hat. If a team draws the letter "G," they must bring back only items that begin with the letter "G." For example, a "P" team might bring back a "pot," a "pickle," a "peanut," a "Ping-pong ball," and so on.

Set a time limit and have a scale handy. When the teams return, award bonus points for various *types* of items: Anything *living* gets 25 extra points (an animal, a plant, a person); anything *weighing* over 25 pounds gets 40 extra points; anything *edible* gets 10 extra points.

Other rules might include these: All items must be obtained for free (no purchases) and with the owner's permission (if the item has an owner). Also, no items may be retrieved from a team member's home or car.

ACTION SCAVENGER HUNT

This is a scavenger hunt for actions rather than objects. Give each team a list of actions. They must go around the neighborhood and find people (one per household) who will perform the designated action. Here's a sample list:

1. Sing two verses of "Old MacDonald Had a Farm."

2. Do 10 jumping jacks.
3. Recite John 3:16.
4. Name five movies currently playing in local theaters.
5. Yodel something.
6. Run around your house.
7. Start your car's engine and honk the horn.
8. Take our picture (with *your* camera).
9. Whistle one verse of "Yankee Doodle."
10. Say the Pledge of Allegiance.
11. Give us a guided tour of your garage.
12. Autograph the bottoms of our feet.
13. Say "bad blood" ten times real fast.
14. Belch.
15. Do a somersault.

Whenever a person performs one of the items on the list, he signs his name under that item to verify he did it. The team with the most signed-off items within the time limit is the winner.

BIGGER AND BETTER HUNT

The results of this popular hunt are incredible. Everyone meets at a central location for instructions. The group is then divided into small hunting groups of four or five, who hunt together on foot, in cars, or whatever way they can. Each group is given a penny to trade up for something better. For example, the group goes to someone's house and asks what in their house, excluding cash, they would trade for the penny. If the item is worth more than the penny, the group trades and thanks the people who made the trade and continues to trade whatever item they have for something bigger and better at the next house. Team members are not allowed to "sweeten the pot" by adding more money to the original penny or any of the items along the way.

Each team has a one-hour limit (or whatever time you decide) and then must return with the last item they traded for. The group with the Biggest and the Best is the winner.

This event has been done successfully with many different groups. Some have traded for such items as washing machines, TV sets (in working condition), even automobiles. The items that are collected can be used later for a rummage sale, or they may be donated to a local service organization.

BIKE RODEO

Here's a super event for junior highers and their bicycles. Have your kids bring their bikes to a large open area for a variety of games like these:

1. *Calf Roping:* One kid stands in the center of an open area, and each contestant tries to "rope the calf" as he rides by on a bicycle. After a rider successfully lassos the person in the middle, he should immediately drop the rope to avoid injury to himself or the calf. The calf may duck, but he must keep his hands at his side and stay on his feet. The fastest time wins.
2. *The 100-Yard Crawl:* Bikes must travel in a straight line to a finish line that is 100 yards away as slowly as possible. If a rider touches a foot or any part of his body to the ground (trying to maintain his balance) or goes off course, he is disqualified. The last person to finish is the winner.
3. *Bike Cross-Country:* This event is an obstacle course that can include anything you want. The rougher the better. From a starting point, bikes compete for time. On the trail, have a Long Jump (a 4-inch log that the bike must jump over), a Tight Rope (a 10-foot-long 2 x 4 that the bike must stay on), a Limbo Branch (low tree branch that the bike rider must go under), a Tire Weave (slalom course made from old tires), and so on.
4. *100-Yard Sprint:* This is a regular 100-yard dash from a standstill with bikes.
5. *Bike Pack:* See how many can fit on a bike and still go ten feet.
6. *Backward Race:* Have the kids who know how to ride a bike backward race down a 100-yard track.
7. *Bike Jousting:* Arm two kids with water balloons. They ride toward each other on two parallel tracks and try to hit the other rider with the water balloon as they ride by.
8. *Barrel Race:* Set up several barrels (or other markers) in a figure-eight course. Bike riders try to ride around the barrels in the fastest time.

9. *Freestyle:* Have kids compete for the most creative, most difficult, most impressive freestyle bike ride. Judges can determine the winners.

DATE SCAVENGER HUNT

Divide into teams and give each one a list of *years* (1987, 1986) from the present year working backward for about thirty years or so. The kids need to collect items that have those years indelibly marked on them. They can bring back license plates, coins, drivers' licenses, books with copyright dates printed on them, deeds, certificates, old magazines, and so on.

This scavenger hunt has one important rule to encourage creativity—only one item per date is allowed. For instance, if the team brings back a *book* for the date 1965, then they cannot use a book for any other date.

DESTINATION UNKNOWN

Have your junior highers meet in the morning for a day of activities that remain a secret to everyone in the group except the youth sponsors. You can include a picnic, an outdoor game, a trip to an amusement park, dinner in a restaurant, a party afterward— whatever your time and budget will allow. Kids enjoy the mystery.

FRISBEE FESTIVAL

This is a good special event for the beach or for an open field, where you have plenty of room. All you need is a supply of Frisbees (available everywhere). Divide the groups into teams and then play the following crazy Frisbee games:
1. *Frisbee Relay:* Team members line up with about twenty feet or so between them. At a signal, the person on one end of the line tosses the Frisbee to the teammate closest to him, who then tosses it to the next person, and so on to the end of the line, and then back again. The first team to get the Frisbee back to the beginning person wins.
2. *Frisbee Distance Relay:* For this one, you need lots of room. The first person on the team throws the Frisbee as far as he can. The next person picks it up where it lands and throws it again from

that point even farther. The next person throws it again and so on. The team that gets the Frisbee the farthest away is the winner.

3. *Frisbee Toss:* Teams of two stand about ten feet away from each other. (There should be two lines of players who stand this distance apart.) At a signal, a frisbee is tossed from one to the other. Then both partners take one step backward, and the Frisbee is tossed again; another step backward, the Frisbee is again tossed, and so on. If the Frisbee is dropped, that pair is out of the game. You must stand in one spot when throwing and catching. Whoever lasts the longest wins.

4. *Team-toss Frisbee:* Two teams line up parallel to each other and about twenty feet apart. The teams face each other and the first person on one team tosses the Frisbee to the first person on the other team, and so on down the line. The thrower's team gets a point if the catcher drops the Frisbee, and the catcher's team scores a point if the thrower tosses the Frisbee beyond the reach of the catcher, who must keep his feet planted. There should be a neutral judge for this game.

5. *Single's Competition:* There are many games designed for individual competition that you can play with Frisbees. Players may throw for distance, throw left-handed (or opposite-handed), throw for accuracy (through a tire or at a target), throw the boomerang shot for accuracy on the return (thrown up and at an angle so that it will return), throw the hot-dogger shot (any spectacular shot—sort of a Frisbee Freestyle judged for originality), and so on.

6. *Other team games:* You can play football, soccer, baseball, and even golf with Frisbees by making up your own rules and by being creative. Have fun!

GIANT LOOKIE

A "lookie" is the name junior highers sometimes give to the gross-looking mess inside someone's mouth when they are eating something and show it to someone else. Unfortunately that's where this idea gets its name.

Everyone brings a can of his favorite condensed soup and a

can of soda pop. After everyone arrives, empty all the cans of soup into one large kettle, add the proper amount of water, then heat. Empty all the soft drinks into another large container. You'll be surprised to find how decent the punch and the soup taste, even when there's only one person who likes cream of asparagus.

GIANT PIZZA BREAKFAST

Here's something that will attract a lot of attention with junior-high kids. Plan a Giant Pizza Breakfast either before church on Sunday or during the week before school. Serve pizza (just use the frozen variety) and soft drinks, and the kids will come. It's a great way to attract kids who wouldn't ordinarily attend your church or youth group functions.

HOT OR COLD CAR RALLY

This car rally is especially good with junior highers as the riders and adult sponsors or parents as the drivers. Only the drivers know the destination, and the passengers give their driver directions. Every five-tenths of a mile (or whatever distance you choose), the driver tells the passengers if they are getting "hot" or "cold" in relationship to the destination. When the car is getting closer to the destination, the driver tells the passengers when they are getting "warmer" or "hotter," and when the car is getting farther away, he tells them that they are getting "cooler," "freezing," and so on. But he cannot tell them anything until they have traveled another five-tenths of a mile. As a variation, the driver can give a clue once every two minutes, no matter how far they have traveled.

To avoid confusion in each car, have the riders elect a spokesperson for the group—the one who gives directions to the driver. All the passengers can have a voice in deciding which way to go, of course, but only the spokesperson can tell the driver where to go.

To avoid cars following each other, schedule each car leaving at intervals of five minutes. The time is recorded when they leave and when they reach the final destination. The best time wins.

175

LATE GREAT SKATE

Here's a special event designed to put new life into the old roller-skating party. Arrange to rent a roller rink for your own private use. Usually you can get one for a flat rate plus skate rentals. Also, make sure you have the freedom to plan your own skating program, rather than being confined to the normal "All Skate," "Couples Only," and "Grand March." You might want to consider an all-night skate that starts around midnight and ends at dawn. Roller rinks are easier to rent at such a ridiculous hour.

Play all sorts of games on skates. Many of your favorite games can be played on skates, giving them an added dimension of fun: races, relays, ball games—all can be done on skates. Just be sure that the games are not too rough to avoid possible injuries.

Some sample roller-skating games:

1. *Rag Tag:* Everyone gets a rag that hangs out of his back pocket or out of his pants. At a signal, everyone starts skating in the same direction, and each skater tries to grab someone else's rag without having his taken by another skater. Once his rag is gone, the skater is out of the race. Awards are given for most rags grabbed by one skater and for whoever stays in the longest.

2. *Obstacle-Course Relay:* Set up an obstacle course for the skaters. The first team to have each of its members skate through it, one-at-a-time, is the winner.

3. *Triple Skate:* Have everyone skate around the rink in threes. No passing is allowed. At a signal, the skater in the middle, or on the right or left, moves up to the next threesome.

4. *Scooter Race:* Have one kid on his haunches who is pushed by another skater. Set a number of laps for the race.

5. *Tumbleweed:* Have all the skaters squat when the music stops or when the whistle blows—quickly very tiring for the skaters.

6. *One-Legged Race:* Skaters race with only one skate. The other foot is used to push.

7. *Run the Gauntlet:* Girls line up in two parallel lines, and boys skate between them with balloons tied to their seats. The girls try to pop the balloons with rolled-up newspapers. A variation is to have three clothespins fastened to each boy's back, and the girls try to grab the clothespins as the boys skate by. Awards are

given to the girl who grabs the most clothespins or pops the most balloons and to the boy who lasts the longest.

8. *London Bridge:* Two skaters stand opposite each other, grab hands, and form a bridge for other skaters to skate under. Each team then lines up and, at a signal, begins skating under the bridge. Once under the bridge, each skater circles around and goes through again, as many times as possible before the time is up. There should be a counter standing by the bridge.

There are many other possibilities, of course. For breathers, you might want to show some films or serve sandwiches and refreshments.

PAPER AIRPLANE DERBY

Here's a simple special event idea that's a lot of fun. Ask all the kids to bring their own paper airplane, made out of anything they want, as long as it is paper. Kids can use paint, glue, and paper, but no wire, wood, or metals. Have an evening of games that feature these creations. Give awards for the best designed airplane, the largest airplane, the smallest airplane, the farthest flight, the plane that stays in the air the longest, the most accurate flight (through a hoop), best landing (onto a runway), and so on.

PERSONALIZED PIZZA PARTY

Provide your junior highers with pizza dough and all the goodies that go on top and let them create their own personal pizzas. Each person gets a lump of dough to shape into a creative design. The only stipulation is that there must be a lip (raised edge), so the sauce won't run off. The pizza can be decorated with olives, mushrooms, cheese, pepperoni, anchovies, and the like. While these creations are being baked, other games can be played. When they are ready, judge them for originality, creativity, and so on. Then, eat up!

SCRIPTURE SCAVENGER HUNT

Here's one that combines a lot of fun with some solid Bible learning. Teams try to bring back items that can be found in the Bible. For example, they might bring back a stick (Moses' rod), or

177

a rock (the stoning of Stephen), or a loaf of bread (the Last Supper). Every item must be accompanied by a Bible verse to prove that it can be found somewhere in the Bible. The team that returns with the most items is the winner.

SUPERSTAR SPECIAL

Here is an activity that is fun to do anytime and can involve all of the kids in some really crazy competition. It is patterned after the "Superstar" events held on television, featuring famous athletes competing in a variety of events to determine who is the best all-round athlete. Normally, there are ten events (or whatever number you choose).

Each participant selects seven events to compete in. If you prefer, you can make everyone compete in all of them, but by giving kids their choice of seven, it helps to equalize things a little bit. In TV's version, only the top three contestants in each event score points, but you may want to allow the top ten in each event to receive points. For example, first place would receive ten points, second place would get nine points, and so on. If someone were to take first place in all seven of his events (very unlikely), he would score seventy points total.

It is best to choose events that do not give a huge advantage to kids who are athletically inclined, older, smarter, or whatever. This way everyone has a chance, and the competition is more fun for everyone involved. Here are some sample events:

1. Water balloon shot put (for distance)
2. Shoe kick (hang shoe loosely on foot and kick it for distance)
3. Baseball hitting (use volleyball or have kids hit wrong-handed)
4. Sack race (in gunnysacks)
5. Paper airplane throwing (for distance in the air)
6. Dart throwing (at dartboard or at balloons)
7. Stilt race (for best time)
8. Joke-telling contest or dramatic-reading contest (judged)
9. Taco eating (who can eat the most in a given time limit)
10. Frisbee throwing (for distance or accuracy)

Of course, you can create your own events to fit your situation. The kids move from event to event and record their scores. At the end, whoever has the highest score (total points) is declared the Superstar and is awarded an appropriate trophy or prize (the crazier the better).

WORLD'S LARGEST BANANA SPLIT

Here's one that a lot of youth groups have done with great success. To make the World's Largest (or Longest) Banana Split, you need to get a long section of house rain gutter. You may have to plug the ends of it to keep it free from leaks. Line the gutter with heavy duty aluminum foil about three times. Now, you're ready to make the banana split. Be sure to obtain enough ice cream, bananas, toppings, nuts, whipped cream, and the like. Arrange to have everyone eat out of the same boat or dip out individual servings into plastic containers, obtained at a local dairy bar. Don't forget to take pictures.

WORLD'S GREATEST FRENCH FRY

Here's an activity that allows your kids to become critics or reviewers of the things they consume. The object is to find the very best French fry in the city. The kids go from one fast-food restaurant to another to try their French fries. For example, they would go to McDonald's, order some French fries, and then divide them up between the group. Each member rates the fries on qualities such as taste, appearance, cost, amount of fries per serving, and saltiness. To add a professional touch, have each member eat a cracker before they taste to "wash the palate." The group's ratings and any additional comments can be shared in the church bulletin. Any common food items work as well.

WORLD'S LARGEST POPCORN BOWL

The next time you plan to have a movie night at your church or if you want to create a refreshment for your next special event, try this. Announce ahead of time that you will have the World's Largest Popcorn Bowl at the activity. The kids will come just to see if you can deliver.

You'll need to get lots of popcorn popped, of course. For the bowl, use a molded plastic, child-sized swimming pool. Just fill it with popcorn, and it will indeed be the world's largest. The kids will love it.

12
CREATIVE LEARNING STRATEGIES FOR JUNIOR-HIGH GROUPS

Listed here is a sampling of outstanding learning strategies for junior highers. They emphasize activity and interaction, involvement and discovery, and issues that junior highers are concerned about. They help kids to learn "experientially," rather than through indoctrination. This method is based on the presupposition that the only learning that significantly affects behavior is that which is self-discovered. Junior highers have a great need to "try things on for size" and to learn in this manner. They don't want to be told what is right and true; they need experiences from which they can learn and opportunities to think for themselves.

The following ideas work well with junior highers. Almost all of them come from the Youth Specialties *Ideas* books (published by Youth Specialties, Inc.) and are used here by permission.

APPENDICES UNITE!

This is a game that would be a great discussion starter about the body of Christ or Christian unity. When the group arrives, give everyone a slip of paper with a part of the body written on it, such as ear, nose, foot, kneecap, hand, or eye. You should try to distribute these, so there will be enough parts to make up two or more complete bodies. In other words, if you have thirty kids, you might want to have three bodies, each with ten parts.

When the signal is given, the kids try to form complete bodies as quickly as possible by getting into groups. The body that gets together first is the winner. A complete body has, of course, only one head, two arms, two legs, and so on. If a body has three legs, then obviously something is wrong.

Once the bodies have formed, you can proceed with some small-group discussion or other activities that require those bodies to work together as a team to simulate how the body of Christ works. An experience like this can help kids to understand passages of Scripture like 1 Corinthians 12 much better.

THE AWARENESS GAME

Begin your session about awareness as follows. Have one person in the group go out of the room for a short time (pick someone who isn't easily embarrassed). Ask the rest of the group to describe what the person was wearing. Be as specific as possible. Then bring the person back in and let everyone see what he was wearing.

Most groups will remember very few specifics about the clothing worn by the chosen person, which proves the shallowness of our everyday contacts with people. Then discuss our ability as Christians to perceive others' needs and show that perception is the first step in ministering to a need—noticing things about others is something that must be worked at. Talk about Christ's perception of needs, how he relied on God the Father for help in this area, and what this means for our ability of perception.

DEAR ABBY

This is a simple yet effective way to give kids the opportunity to really minister to each other. It also provides you with insight into the concerns and problems of individuals in your junior-high group.

Each person is given a piece of paper and pencil. The kids are instructed to write a "Dear Abby" letter to explain an unresolved problem that they have to a newspaper columnist, such as Abby or Ann Landers. The letter can be signed "Confused," "Frustrated," or with any name other than the real one.

After everyone has finished, collect the papers and redistribute them so that everyone has someone else's letter. Each person now becomes Abby or Ann Landers and writes a helpful answer or solution to the problem. Allow plenty of time. When the answers are completed, collect the papers once again.

Now read the letters to the group, one-at-a-time, along with the answers. Discuss them by asking the group whether or not the advice given was good or bad. Other solutions to the problem can be suggested by the group. There is an excellent chance that the kids will be able to give sincere, sensible, and practical help to each other.

DECISION

Give each person five or ten minutes to decide which of the following things they consider to be the most harmful. Their job is to rank each item by writing the number 1 by what they think is the most harmful; number 2 by the second most harmful, and so on. Afterward, discuss the results. Define "harmful" as it relates to all areas of life.

_____ Getting drunk

_____ Moderate drinking (alcohol)

_____ Lack of exercise

_____ Cigarette smoking

_____ Not going to church

_____ Poor eating habits (types of food, how eaten)

_____ Marijuana

_____ Drugs (amphetamines, LSD)

_____ Watching too much TV

_____ Lack of medical attention when necessary

_____ Premarital sex

_____ Nervous anxiety and tension

_____ Fatigue, caused by never getting enough sleep

_____ Overeating

_____ Cheating on exams at school

ENGLISH TEST

The following exercise is a fun way to show kids how we often make judgments too hastily. Distribute copies of the following paragraph and ask each person to make the corrections as instructed. When they are finished, follow up with a discussion about Matthew 7:1–6.

183

Divide this paragraph into sentences using capitals at the beginning of sentences, periods at the end of sentences, and commas or other punctuation where needed. Once begun, *do not go back* and try to correct.

He is a young man yet experienced in vice and wickedness he is never found in opposing the works of iniquity he takes delight in the downfall of his neighbors he never rejoices in the prosperity of his fellow-creatures he is always ready to assist in destroying the peace of society he takes no pleasure in serving the Lord he is uncommonly diligent in sowing discord among his friends and acquaintances he takes no pride in laboring to promote the cause of Christianity he has not been negligent in endeavoring to tear down the church he makes no effort to subdue his evil passions he strives hard to build up Satan's kingdom he lends no aid to the support of the gospel among heathen he contributes largely to the Devil he will never go to heaven he must go where he will receive his just reward.

Here is the way it should be corrected:

He is a young man, yet experienced. In vice and wickedness, he is never found. In opposing the works of iniquity, he takes delight. In the downfall of his neighbors, he never rejoices. In the prosperity of his fellow-creatures, he is always ready to assist. In destroying the peace of society, he takes no pleasure. In serving the Lord, he is uncommonly diligent. In sowing discord among his friends and acquaintances, he takes no pride. In laboring to promote the cause of Christianity, he has not been negligent. In endeavoring to tear down the church, he makes no effort. To subdue his evil passions, he strives hard. To build up Satan's kingdom, he lends no aid. To the support of the gospel among heathen, he contributes largely. To the Devil he will never go. To heaven he must go, where he will receive his just reward.

FOTO-MATCH

Hang up twenty or so photos of people of all kinds—old, young, black, white, attractive, ugly, fat, slim, wealthy, poor. The first week the pictures are displayed, ask each kid to write a description of each person according to the picture. Collect them and combine all the individual descriptions into a concise paragraph that accurately reflects the group consensus of each picture. Attach the descriptions to each picture for the next meeting. Tell the kids to look at the photos and the descriptions carefully (make sure they are numbered) and then answer the following questions:

1. Choose five people you would want to work with for one year. Why?
2. Is there any one person you would not want anything to do with? Why?
3. Who, if any, would you be willing to go out on a date with?
4. Who, if any, would you worship with?
5. Which person do you think you could really like? Why?

For a variation, ask the kids to answer the questions again as their parents would. And, of course, you can also make up other questions equally as good as these.

GIVE-AND-GET GAME

Have everyone reach into his pocket or purse and produce a small amount of change. Any amount will do. It works best when people use real money, but if they don't have any, you could give them some or use play money. The game involves three rounds, with each round lasting one minute

The first round is a *giving* round. Announce that when the signal is given, the kids should try to give away as much money as they can. The second round is a *getting* round. During this round, the kids should try to get as much money as possible. There are no rules for how you give or get money. The third round is optional. It can be either a *giving* or *getting* round. Let them vote with a show of hands and then do whichever they decide.

After this short but active game, there will be lots of possibilities for discussion. Some sample questions are these:
1. How many kids came out ahead? How many lost money?
2. Which round did you enjoy the most? Why?
3. How did you feel during the *getting* round? During the *giving* round.
4. Did *greed* enter into this game?
5. Did you place a limit on how much you were going to give?
6. Did you have a strategy for getting?
7. What did you learn about giving from this game?

GOSPEL NEWSPAPER

Here's an idea that gets everybody involved and allows kids to think through and express what they consider to be the important tenets of the Christian faith.

You might begin by scheduling a field trip or visit to your local newspaper, just to get the feel for newspaper publishing and journalism. Then, propose to the group that they publish one issue of a newspaper containing editorials, articles, poems, song lyrics, cartoons, pictures, interviews, drawings, and scriptures to communicate some of the most important aspects of Christianity to a person who knows nothing about it. The project might begin with a discussion of some of the foundational and representative truths of Christianity and how these might be expressed in printed form to an unbeliever; for example, "How can we communicate the centrality of Christ himself in our paper so if a person who is unfamiliar with Christianity reads this paper, he/she might come to some understanding of what it's all about?"

The paper can be written, typed, or printed on an offset press—whatever the class decides. Your local paper may even publish it for you. The length of the project can vary with the elaborateness of the design of the paper and the interest of the group. The various phases of the operation can allow individuals to work on a job that most interests them: photographer, writer, poet, artist, typist, reporter. The very act of discussing the essence of the Christian faith and actually having to "put something down on paper" can be a faith-building and enlightening experience.

THE GOSSIP GAME

The Scriptures have a great deal to say about the consequences of idle gossip or "murdering with the tongue." The following game is useful as a way of pointing out the seriousness of spreading rumors.

Choose three young people to leave the room while a fourth person copies (as well as he can) on a poster board a picture that he is shown.

One of the three persons outside comes in and draws the same drawing, using the first person's drawing as the guide, rather than the original.

The next person comes in and draws his drawing from the second person's and likewise with the last person.

The last person's drawing is then compared with the original, and of course, there will hardly be any resemblance to the original at all, since each of the young people copied each other's, and everyone changed the drawing a little, usually omitting or adding important things.

This game is entertaining as well as revealing, and it can be followed up with a discussion about gossip and communication.

THE GREAT BUTTON CONTROVERSY

As a discussion starter about conformity, put ten or twelve buttons in a box and pass them around the group. Have each student count the buttons and remember how many were in the box. By prior arrangement, the next-to-last person removes one button from the box secretly, so that the last person's count is off by one. When you ask the kids how many they counted, everyone will agree except for that one person (hopefully). In all probability, the last person will change his count to conform to the others, even though he is sure he is right. Follow up with a discussion of group pressure and how we often deny our personal convictions to be accepted by the group.

HOW GOD SEES ME

Each person is asked to take a sheet of newsprint and on one side draw pictures, cartoons, or sayings expressing "How I See God." The other side is to be filled with symbols expressing "How I Think God Sees Me." Allow twenty to twenty-five minutes to complete. After everyone is finished, each person should explain his drawing to the entire group. This exercise helps the group share where each one stands with God at present and demonstrates the varying facets of an individual's experience with God.

HUMAN CONTINUUM

When discussing subjects that have many points of view, have the kids arrange themselves (prior to the discussion) on a human continuum from one extreme viewpoint to the opposite extreme. For example, if you are discussing drinking, have the kids line up with all those who are for drinking on one end, and those who are against it at the other. Undecideds or moderates would be somewhere in the middle.

187

For	Against

Kids may discuss the issue among themselves as they attempt to find the right spot in the line in relationship to each other. After they are settled, further discussion or debate can take place as kids attempt to defend their positions. Anyone may change positions at any time.

THE LABOR GAME

This game is based on the parable of the householder (Matt. 20:1–16). This sometimes perplexing story can become real by allowing your youth to experience the frustration of the workers who complained about equal pay at the end of the day, even though some did not work as long or as hard as others. The owner (God) was just and kept his promise—paying exactly what he said he would. This would have satisfied the workers until greed crept in. The following simulation game will help kids to understand this parable more fully.

As the kids enter the room, have various puzzles, brainteasers, or skills displayed on several tables. Some should be very easy; others, impossible. Assign points for each puzzle—depending on the difficulty, and each person keeps his own score. After twenty or thirty minutes, call a halt. Go to each young person, ask how many points he has, and then reach into a bag and give him a prize. The prize can be very small; just be sure every prize is exactly the same for everyone.

As you do this, it will soon be obvious to everyone in the group what is happening. No matter how high or low the score, they are all receiving equal payment. Allow free talk as you distribute the reward. Follow up with discussion questions, such as: How do you honestly feel? What is your attitude toward the prize-giver? How do you feel toward the other young people? Ask

188

the person who scored the highest and the person who scored the lowest how they feel. Follow by reading the Scripture account of the parable and discuss greed, envy, lust, and competition, and how these can cloud one's relationship with God.

LAMED VOVNIK CONVENTION

A charming Jewish legend states that the world exists due to the presence of only thirty-six righteous people. The Jewish name for these people is *lamed vov* (pronounced "lahmed vov")—"thirty-six." These people may be of any station in life, poor or mighty, men or women, hermits or public figures. The only thing we know about them is that they are alive and that they do not know that they are lamed vovniks. If they claim to be, then they cannot be.

To conduct a Lamed Vovnik convention, divide your group into as many small groups as you wish, and have each group nominate several individuals outside your youth group whom they think might qualify as a lamed vovnik. They should be righteous, selfless, and the kind of persons on whom the welfare of the world might rest. Give each group ten to fifteen minutes for this, and set a maximum number of people whom each group may nominate.

When the groups have finished, have a nominating convention. Each group announces their choices and explains why they nominated whom they did. A list can be kept on a blackboard, and a final vote can be taken to arrive at the entire group's guesses for who the thirty-six lamed vovniks are.

Many famous people will undoubtedly be nominated, but the beauty of the exercise is that many ordinary people, not well-known, will undoubtedly be favorites. Perhaps the best thing about this activity is the shift of emphasis from fame to humility. True models begin to emerge, and kids begin to put some handles on what righteousness is all about.

LIFE AUCTION

Print up or display the following list of life options and give each person an equal amount of money (play money or poker chips). Then have an auction, in which the kids try to acquire as many of the items on the list as they feel they want and can afford.

Once their money is gone, they can bid on nothing else. Give the kids the time to decide and set their priorities before the bidding begins. You can add more items to the list if necessary. If you have more kids than items, sell each item twice. Or have the kids get into small groups, decide what they want, and then bid in groups. It's a great way to start a discussion about what is important in life and what is not.

Life Options

1. To have a wonderful family life without any hassles.
2. To have all the money I need to be happy.
3. Never to be sick.
4. To find the right mate, who is beautiful and fulfills me.
5. Never to have pimples.
6. To be able to do whatever I want whenever I want.
7. To have all the power the president has.
8. To be the best-looking person in the world.
9. To have a real hunger to read the Bible faithfully.
10. To be able to understand all things.
11. To eliminate all hunger and disease in the world.
12. To be close to God always.
13. Never to feel lonely or put down.
14. To be happy and peaceful always.
15. Never to feel hurt.
16. To own a beautiful home, car, boat, and plane.
17. To be supersmart without ever having to attend school.
18. To be able to excel quickly and to be superior in all things.
19. To be filled with God's presence in the most dynamic way.
20. To know that you are always in God's will.
21. To be the greatest athlete in the world.
22. To be looked up to by everyone else.
23. To become a star on TV.
24. To have a lot of close friends who never let you down.
25. To walk close to God.

LIFE LETTERS

Following a discussion about suicide, have kids write a life letter to a potential suicide victim to express their reasons for believing that life is worth living. After about twenty minutes of writing, have the kids share their letters with the rest of the group (if they want to). This gives some people a chance to share their faith and provide a unique learning experience as well.

MALL MANIA

This activity makes an excellent discussion about accepting other people as they are. Divide your group into small groups of four to five each. Give them written instructions to help them observe people at a mall. For example, they could be instructed to count how many people they see who are fat, or how many are skinny, short, tall, ugly, beautiful, clean, dirty, well-dressed, or slobs. Also have them describe the two people they liked the most and the two they liked the least.

After a few hours of observation, meet in a central location at the mall or back at your church for a discussion of God's acceptance of all people. Have the kids share results from their views of the people at the mall. Tie it together by asking questions about God's acceptance. James 2:1–13 can be used as Scripture for this discussion.

THE MORAL OF THE STORY

Read a story (proverb or fable, biblical or make-believe) and omit the moral at the end, if there is one. Challenge each person to write what he thinks the moral of the story would be. They can then share them and discuss. It's amazing how many different things you can learn from one simple story.

PARABLE OF THE SOWER

Here's a good way to help your junior highers understand the Parable of the Sower a little better. Using a plant starter box, fill each tray with one of the four types of soils mentioned in the parable: hard, dry soil; soil with rocks in it; soil with weeds in it (grass seed can be used); and good soil. Discuss the parable with the group, and speculate about how the various kinds of soils might affect the growth of a plant.

Next, plant some seeds in the four different soils. Corn seed will work fine. Make sure someone is in charge of watering the plantings as required over the next few weeks, and let the plants grow. As the weeks go by, you can chart the progress of the plants and draw comparisons to the principles taught by Jesus in the parable. It takes approximately eighty days for corn to grow, so you might want to take some pictures at weekly intervals just to keep track of how they're doing. The pictures would make a nice poster at the conclusion of the experiment.

You can transplant the good corn into a garden when it's ready, and maybe even eat the corn with the group. They'll never forget the parable.

PENNY FOR YOUR THOUGHTS

Many times it is difficult to get junior highers talking in a discussion. This idea may be just the extra inspiration your kids need to get the verbal juices going.

Ask each of the kids to bring twenty pennies and a nickel for the next discussion (topical or general sharing of ideas). The kids sit in a circle around a pot. The leader poses a question, and each person in the circle tosses in a "penny for his/her thoughts" on the subject. If someone wants to interject a statement (more than just a sentence), it is called "putting in your two cents worth," and the person must put in two cents. If a person cannot think of anything to say when it's their turn (and there are only a few of those, believe it or not), he/she may "four-feit" by putting four cents in the pot. A person can "four-feit" only once and does so by throwing in a nickel and getting back a penny.

When the discussion is over, the money collected can go to a worthy cause, or you can award the pot of pennies to the "poor kid" who talked too much.

PERFECT PAIR

For a good discussion starter about the family, try this one. Simply tell kids that they are to invent the world's most nearly

Call for fast service:
(619) 440-2333

NO POSTAGE
NECESSARY
IF MAILED
IN THE
UNITED STATES

BUSINESS REPLY MAIL
FIRST CLASS   PERMIT NO. 16   EL CAJON, CA

POSTAGE WILL BE PAID BY ADDRESSEE

YOUTH SPECIALTIES
1224 Greenfield Dr.
El Cajon, CA 92021-9989

Il|....l.lll....l.l....lll.l.l.l.l.l.l.l....lll

Call for fast service:
(619) 440-2333

NO POSTAGE
NECESSARY
IF MAILED
IN THE
UNITED STATES

BUSINESS REPLY MAIL
FIRST CLASS   PERMIT NO. 16   EL CAJON, CA

POSTAGE WILL BE PAID BY ADDRESSEE

YOUTH SPECIALTIES
1224 Greenfield Dr.
El Cajon, CA 92021-9989

Il|....l.lll....l.l....lll.l.l.l.l.l.l.l....lll

The People Who Brought You This Book...

Invite you to discover MORE valuable youth ministry resources.

Youth Specialties offers an assortment of books, publications, tapes and events, all designed to encourage and train youth workers and their kids. Just check what you're interested in below and return this card, and we'll send you FREE information on our products and services.

Please send me FREE information I've checked below:

☐ The Complete Youth Specialties Catalog of Youth Ministry Books and Products

Event Brochures:

☐ The National Youth Workers Convention

☐ The National Resource Seminar for Youth Workers

☐ "Grow For It" High School Events

☐ "On the Edge" Junior High Events

☐ "Understanding Your Teenager" Seminars for Parents

☐ "Riptide" Summer High School Conferences

Name _____

Address _____

City _____ State _____ Zip _____

The People Who Brought You This Book...

Invite you to discover MORE valuable youth ministry resources.

Youth Specialties offers an assortment of books, publications, tapes and events, all designed to encourage and train youth workers and their kids. Just check what you're interested in below and return this card, and we'll send you FREE information on our products and services.

Please send me FREE information I've checked below:

☐ The Complete Youth Specialties Catalog of Youth Ministry Books and Products

Event Brochures:

☐ The National Youth Workers Convention

☐ The National Resource Seminar for Youth Workers

☐ "Grow For It" High School Events

☐ "On the Edge" Junior High Events

☐ "Understanding Your Teenager" Seminars for Parents

☐ "Riptide" Summer High School Conferences

Name _____

Address _____

City _____ State _____ Zip _____

perfect couple, that is, the man and woman best suited to create the ideal home and family and most likely to be happy. Divide into small groups and ask them to describe their perfect couple. Things to consider:

1. The couple themselves:
   a. background
   b. age
   c. education
   d. religious affiliation
   e. race
   f. political views

2. Their lifestyle:
   a. jobs (employment)
   b. hobbies
   c. sex life
   d. leisure time
   e. entertainment
   f. habits
   g. friends and associations

3. Their possessions:
   a. money
   b. furniture
   c. house and neighborhood
   d. books, magazines
   e. appliances
   f. recreational needs
   g. auto(s)

4. Philosophy about child rearing:
   a. discipline
   b. education
   c. manners
   d. dress
   e. independence

The items listed are only suggestions, and kids should not be limited to them. After a twenty- or thirty-minute period of working in their groups, have each group describe their perfect couple. Make lists on the blackboard or use an overhead projector. Compare each group's description of their couple.

Discuss the differences and similarities and ask why certain characteristics occur more often than others. Talk about prejudices and relate it to Scripture. What matters and what doesn't? Also discuss the interaction that took place in each small group—the disputes, differences of opinion, and so forth. A lot of healthy discussion can come from this exercise.

THE POOR MAN'S HOLY LAND TOUR

You can have a Holy Land tour without actually going there, simply by escorting your junior highers to places within walking or driving distance that resemble biblical locations. This could include taking them to the tallest building in town and having a Bible study there about Satan tempting Jesus to jump from the high mountain. It might also include a trip to the city jail where you could talk about Paul's imprisonment. The options are endless: A Jewish synagogue, a mountainside (for the Sermon on the Mount), a garden (for the Garden of Gethsemane), an upstairs room (for the Last Supper), an old boiler room (for the story of the Hebrew children in the fiery furnace), on a country road (for the story of Paul's Damascus-road experience), a lakefront, or a wilderness area (depending on where you live). Doing something like this as a visual aid is worth a thousand flannelgraphs.

PRAYER CANDLES

This idea will help your junior highers to pray together more effectively, and pray for each other. Have the entire group sit in a circle (in a darkened room or outdoors at night) with everyone holding a candle. One candle is lit, then the person holding that candle silently or aloud prays for one other member of the group in the circle (preferably someone across the circle). After completing the prayer, that person goes over to the person he just prayed for and lights that person's candle, then returns to his seat with the lighted candle. The one whose candle was just lit then prays for another in the circle and does the same thing. This continues until all the candles are lit and the leader closes in prayer. All the candles can be blown out simultaneously. The symbolism involved can be very meaningful.

PROGRESSIVE WORSHIP SERVICE

Here's an interesting way to involve young people in worship. It can be done in a church, in homes, or on a weekend retreat. There really is no limit to its possibilities. It works just like a progressive dinner.

A worship service has a variety of elements, just like a dinner does. By taking each element of worship separately and in a different location, it provides a good opportunity to teach young people about these elements of worship. Acts 2:42 and Colossians 3:16 provide a good scriptural base. Here's one way to do it:

1. *Fellowship:* Begin with some kind of group interaction or sharing that provides a chance for the kids to get to know one another better. Something that would put the kids in a celebrative, not rowdy, mood would be appropriate.
2. *Spiritual Songs:* At the next location, have someone lead the group in a variety of well-known hymns and favorite songs of worship.
3. *Prayer:* Move to another location that provides a good atmosphere for prayer. If outside, a garden would be nice, as Jesus often chose a garden for prayer. Have the kids offer prayer requests and thanksgivings and have several kids lead in prayer.
4. *Scripture Reading:* At the next location have several kids read a lesson from the Old Testament, the New Testament, and perhaps the Psalms. Use a modern English translation.
5. *Teaching:* The next stop can be where the sermon is preached. If you prefer not to be "preachy," substitute a dialogue sermon, a film, or something of that nature.
6. *Breaking of Bread (Communion):* The last stop can be around the Lord's Table, with a communion service. Conduct this however you choose, but it should be a time of celebration.

There are other ingredients that go into worship (like the offering) that you can incorporate into the others or take separately.

Design your own progressive worship service, and you can be sure that your group will never forget it.

QUICKIES
One easy way to get kids to be open and to express themselves on a particular topic is to give them "quickies"—"finish this sentence" phrases they must respond to. They can either be written out by each person secretly on cards, collected, and read back to the group by the leader, or they can be discussed in small groups. If you use the latter method, have the kids get into groups of four and share their answers with each other, one-at-a-time. It's not only a good way to get kids thinking, but it also encourages communication among group members. Allow kids the freedom to pass if a question is too hard to answer. Here are a few sample Quickies that you might be able to use.
1. I am proud of . . .
2. I wish I were . . .
3. I wish I were not . . .
4. I wish I had . . .
5. I wish I had not . . .
6. I wish I could . . .
7. I fear most . . .
8. My favorite place is . . .
9. I wish my parents would . . .
10. If I had a hundred dollars, I would . . .
11. I hate . . .
12. My hero is . . .
13. The hardest thing for me to do is . . .
14. I am really happy when . . .
15. If I were God, I would . . .

ROBIN HOOD
Here's a fun simulation game that can start some good discussion on the subjects of giving, selfishness, anger, relationships, and more. Divide into three groups. One group is the Givers; another, the Takers; and the third, the Robin Hoods.
Give everyone in the room five clip-on clothespins and have

them fasten them onto their clothes anywhere they want, as long as they're visible. When the signal is given, each group moves about the room doing as its name implies. If you're a Giver, then you give the clothespins you have to others of your choice. If you're a Taker, then you take. If you're a Robin Hood, then you try to "right the wrongs" that are being done by stealing from the rich and giving to the poor.

After a few minutes, discuss what happened within the group with questions such as these: How did you like your particular role in the game? Did anything in the game seem unfair? Did you get angry? Did you ever want to change roles? How does this game compare with real life? Are there any real-life Robin Hoods around today?

ROCK MUSIC COUNCIL

This idea deals with rock music and its effect upon young people. Very often the trend in churches is either to forbid rock music (burn the records) or to ignore the whole issue. Probably the saner approach is to allow kids the chance to evaluate the music and make a decision for themselves.

Get a few volunteers in your youth group to form a Rock Music Council, who will once a month listen to the current Top 20 records and evaluate them carefully. The records can be taped, purchased, borrowed, or whatever. Sometimes, it is possible to get the records free from a local radio station, which usually has lots of records. Get the lyrics (if possible) and rate the songs in areas such as musical appeal, word content, values of the song (compared to Christian values), hidden meanings (if any), and so on. The results can be shared with the total group, and the kids can decide how to respond. You can get a lot of mileage out of something like this in terms of discussion and interest.

ROLE BOWL

Print up the following situations on cards and put them in a bowl. Divide into small groups and let each person pick one card and think about it. Ask the kids to share their solutions to the situation. (The more verbal kids will obviously share first. *But don't force anyone to share!)* After each person finishes, allow others in the group to comment or add their own thoughts.

1. I don't get it. If Christianity is true, how come there are so many religions that call themselves Christian? I mean, what's the difference between Baptists, Presbyterians, and all the others?
2. If you ask me, the Christian religion makes you a "doormat"—always loving and turning the other cheek.
3. What if I lived like a nonbeliever for eighty years and then became a Christian on my deathbed? Would Billy Graham and I go to the same place?
4. I have been reading through the Old Testament for English class. How come God ordered his people to kill everybody—even women and children—when they conquered a land? What kind of a God is that?
5. Your mother and I do not believe in all this Jesus stuff and we think you spend too much time in church. So we want you to stay away from church for a while.
6. If God exists, then how come you can't see him—or it? Why don't you prove that God exists? Go ahead—prove it to me.
7. The Bible has some nice little stories in it, but everyone knows it's full of contradictions, errors, and just plain myths. How can you believe it?
8. I know a bunch of people who go to your church and they are supposed to be Christians, but I also know what they do during the week and at parties that I go to. They are phonies. If Christianity is so great, how come so many phonies?
9. My little brother died of leukemia and I prayed like crazy. Don't tell me there is a God who loves us. How come he didn't help my brother?
10. Look, I know I am overweight and even though it hurts me to say it, I'm ugly. And I started coming to your church because I thought kids in your youth group would treat me differently than the kids at school. Wrong! They ignore me and make fun of me just like everyone else. How come?

RUN FOR YOUR LIFE

Although this strategy deals with the subject of death, it is really about life and how we live it. The purpose of this exercise is to help young people evaluate their priorities in light of what is really important. It allows the group to contrast what they are doing now with what they would do if they had only one month to live. Give each person in the group a list similar to the one below.

If I only had one month to live, I would:

_____ perform some high-risk feat that I had always wanted to do, figuring that if I didn't make it, it wouldn't really matter.

_____ stage an incredible robbery for a large amount of money, which I would immediately give to the needy and starving of the world.

_____ not tell anyone.

_____ use my dilemma to present the gospel to many people as well as I could.

_____ spend all my time in prayer and Bible reading.

_____ make my own funeral arrangements.

_____ offer myself to science or medicine for high-risk experiments.

_____ have as much fun as possible (sex, parties, booze, whatever turns me on).

_____ travel around the world and see as much as possible.

_____ buy lots of stuff I have always wanted on credit, such as expensive cars, fancy clothes, exotic food. ("Sorry, the deceased left no forwarding address.")

_____ spend my last month with my family or close friends.

_____ not do anything much different, just go on as always.

_____ isolate myself from everyone, find a remote place and meditate.

_____ write a book about my life (or last month).

_____ sell all my possessions and give the money to my family, friends, or others who need it.

_____ try to accomplish as many worthwhile projects as possible.

_____ (your idea) _____

Then have the group rank these alternatives (plus any they wish to add). The first item on their list would be the one they would most likely do, and the last would be the one they would least likely do. Have everyone share their choices, explain why they chose that way, and then discuss the results with the entire group. Another way to evaluate the alternatives is to put each one on a continuum. One end of the continuum would be "Yes definitely" and the other end would be "Absolutely not." After each alternative is placed on the continuum, compare and discuss that alternative with the rest of the group.

SENSE SCRIPTURES

Here's a good way to add a new dimension to your next Bible study or lesson that involves a Bible passage. To begin, read the passage to the group and then explain that you are going to read it again while they (the group) close their eyes and tell you what they "sense" from the story or situation. In other words, you want them to put themselves into the actual scene of the incident being described as you read. Then they are to tell you what they see, hear, smell, taste, and feel. With the active imaginations that most kids have, the results should be exciting.

For example, when Jesus calmed the storm in Matthew 8, responses might sound like this:

SEE—dark clouds, lightning, big waves, sea gulls
HEAR—thunder, splashing, men shouting, boat creaking
TASTE—water, salt, cottonmouth (fear), lunch coming up
FEEL—seasick, the boat rocking, the humidity, the cold
SMELL—rain, salt, wet people who smell bad anyway, fish

On the "feel" part, you might want to consider *emotional* feelings as well—fear, anger (because Jesus was sleeping), confusion, frustrations. This approach can really help young people to relate to the Bible in a fresh and intimate way.

SHOPPING SPREE

For a creative look at money and how people spend it, here is a simple simulation to try with your junior highers. Buy or print several million dollars in play money. Then, divide it into random amounts ($3,000 to $450,000) placed in plain envelopes. Pass out these envelopes to your group.

Now for the shopping spree. Set up a table or bulletin board with a wide assortment of full-page advertisements for things like cars, mansions, computers, vacations, food, savings accounts, and Christian relief efforts. Each youth gets an order blank to buy any items they wish, as long as they can pay for them by themselves or by pooling their money. Give them ten minutes to shop and five minutes to fill in their order blanks.

Gather all of the order blanks, or compile a blackboard list of everything ordered. Discuss the values expressed, their feelings about unequal distribution of the cash, and their responsibility to care for the needy.

STONE AN ATHEIST

This is a unique way to see how secure your kids are in the Christian walk. It will expose them to hidden attitudes they may have toward people who don't call themselves "Christian." It will also show them their need to understand how to witness, and the importance of having a working knowledge of Scripture.

To begin, you must recruit someone who is a Christian to role play an atheist. Whoever this person is, he must not be known by any of the kids. The person should be prepared to speak for fifteen minutes about why he doesn't believe in God. Areas to be included in the speech could be these:

1. The problem of evil in the world
2. Hypocrisy in the church
3. How church history is filled with brutality and war in the name of God
4. Evolution and other theories of science that contradict Scripture
5. The church's seeming unconcern for the ills of society
6. The existence of many different religions in a variety of cultures

You may even tell the kids that you have invited an atheist to speak on the subject of "Why I don't believe in God." After the speech, ask the speaker to have a discussion period, with questions from the kids. Now sit back and watch the stones be thrown! Be sure to take notes on the kids' reactions to this "atheist." Don't talk or get involved yourself.

Stop the discussion after about fifteen minutes and reveal the secret. Now you can lead a discussion with some of the following questions:

1. What was your attitude toward the atheist when you couldn't answer him/her during the speech?
2. Did you feel frustrated over not being able to give an adequate answer to all the problems he/she mentioned?
3. Was there any truth in some of his/her complaints? If so, how did you feel about it?
4. What should the church be doing in society to minister to its ills?
5. What about the problem of hypocrisy in the church?
6. How can we minister in love to those around us who don't believe in God?

TEN YEARS FROM NOW

Here's a fun exercise to get kids thinking about the future. Print the following on a half sheet of paper and let the kids complete the statement. If your group is shy, don't have them put their names on the paper and discuss the answers as a group. If your kids don't mind sharing their responses, then go around the group and discuss each one individually.

Ten Years From Now . . .

1. My height: _____
2. My weight: _____
3. My hair style: _____
4. Where I will be living: _____
5. What I will be doing: _____
6. Dreams and goals I will have: _____
7. I feel I will have been a success in life if: _____
8. I will look back on this year as a year of: _____

THANKSGIVING EXCHANGE

This is a good discussion starter for Thanksgiving or for any time when you want to teach a lesson about gratitude. It works best with a group that knows each other fairly well. Begin by having each person share one or two things that they are thankful for. These will usually be the kind of things that are most obvious to them.

KRISTEN
can be thankful for:
1. Having a sister
2. Good health
3 Doesn't need glasses
4. Has lots of friends
5. Got a summer job

Then have each person write his name on the top of a sheet of paper. Collect the sheets and redistribute them so that everyone has a sheet with someone else's name on it. Now have each person write on that sheet what he would be thankful for if he were the person whose name is on that sheet. They can list as many things as they want. Pass the sheets back to the person whose name is on each sheet and discuss the following questions:

1. What things are written on your sheet that you haven't thanked God for lately?

2. What things are written on your sheet that you had never even thought about thanking God for?

3. Is anything written on your sheet that you disagree with? That you don't think you should be thankful for?

This exercise helps young people realize that they often take for granted many things that they should be thankful for.

A TOUR OF YOUR LIFE

This day-long field trip is great with junior highers and gives them an opportunity to view life somewhat more completely and realistically. Begin by visiting the maternity ward of a local hospital (prearranged, of course) where the kids can see newborns and their parents. Perhaps a doctor can tell about the birth process. Next, take the kids to a local college or university campus and show them around. The next stop should be a factory or shop. At this point, the need for work and the types of work available can be discussed.

Then visit with older folks in a convalescent home or some other place where senior citizens live. Allow the kids to share with them in some way and allow the seniors to share with the kids. The last stop on the tour should be a mortuary or funeral home. The funeral director may show the kids around, explain what happens to the corpse when it is brought in, the types of caskets available, and so on. Close the experience with a meeting or discussion in the funeral chapel (if there is one) or elsewhere if you wish. Other places can be added to this tour depending on how much time you have or the types of places available to you. Allow kids to think about the kind of life they want and how they are going to achieve their goals.

13.
SERVICE PROJECTS FOR JUNIOR-HIGH GROUPS

Junior highers need to be given opportunities to express their faith in practical and meaningful ways. They also need to feel the sense of accomplishment and self-worth that comes from serving others and from getting involved in worthwhile activities that demonstrate to others the love of Christ. Service projects like the ones that follow work very well with junior highers to help fulfill those needs. They are especially good because they do not require long-term commitments from the kids, which often tend to frustrate them. These projects may be accomplished in a relatively short period of time and with good results.

It is important for junior highers to understand that the gospel is not just words, but also action. Too often love is talked about in the church without the necessary emphasis on doing it. Service projects are simple yet practical ways to help kids put a handle on their faith and turn Christian love into real, significant action. Junior highers are fully capable of following through and usually will get very excited about the possibilities of service projects.

The following games are just a few of the many possibilities for putting faith into action.

ADOPT-A-GARDEN

Here's an idea that can really "grow" on you. Invite your group to adopt the gardens of shut-in, chronically ill, hospitalized, or aged people. Supply the seeds and encourage the youth to supply the tools and muscle power. They can prepare the soil, plant, cultivate, and ultimately harvest the vegetables for the people who own the gardens and who, of course, are unable to do the work. It makes for great interaction between the generations! Especially helpful are youth who are into farming, biology, and the "back-to-the-earth" movement.

An adaptation of this idea involves others in the congregation. While publicizing "Adopt-a-Garden," invite others who already have gardens to set aside one or two rows for giving the harvest to the hungry. Again, youth can supply the seeds and, after the harvest, can deliver the food to the needy. This can fit well into a long-range hunger-awareness program.

CONVALESCENT-HOME MINISTRY

Arrange with one or more of the convalescent homes in your area for a group of junior highers to come and minister in some way to the patients on a regular basis. As a group, the kids can put on special programs or they may minister in a more direct way, such as by reading to people who have lost much of their vision, helping them to write letters, feeding them, or similar tasks as directed by the convalescent home director. Most convalescent homes welcome this kind of involvement by youth groups and, of course, the experience is a valuable one for the kids. If you have a home for retarded children in your area, the same kind of ministry can be done there. Junior highers should be exposed to people who are less fortunate to develop a healthy concern and respect for them.

GOLF CLUB WASHING

Here's a unique fund raiser that gets good results. Set up a booth at the eighteenth green of a local golf course and offer to wash golf clubs for the tired hackers. All you need is permission from the golf course pro (or park board for municipal courses), a pail of soapy water, a brush, a pail of clean water, a coin collector, and a few towels. For extra service, you may want to wax the woods and use metal polish on the irons. When the money is going to a worthy cause, most golfers will be glad to pay a reasonable price.

GROUP GARAGE SALES

Garage sales are big business these days. There are actually professional garage-sale shoppers who do nothing but go to all the sales in town each week to look for bargains. Invite the people in the congregation to donate all kinds of unwanted but sellable items to the junior-high group and then borrow someone's garage for a Saturday and schedule a garage sale. Put an ad in the local paper, and post lots of directional signs. Price each item low enough that it will sell easily, and the results will be surprising. The money can then be used for a worthy cause of your choosing.

LET IT GROWL

This is a combination "Lock In" and "Starve-a-thon" designed to raise money for Third World countries and to sensitize kids to the problem of world hunger. The group meets together on a Friday evening and remains together until the following evening, participating in a fast—going without food for at least twenty-four hours. During this time, there are many games, simulations, films, and other activities that can be used to focus on the hunger issue. The kids are also encouraged to obtain sponsors prior to the event; the sponsor pays a certain amount of money (as much as possible) for each hour the person is able to go without food. The money is then collected and contributed to a relief agency that is helping to supply food to undernourished people around the world.

One relief agency, World Vision (919 W. Huntington Drive, Monrovia, Calif. 91016), has creatively organized this program and has it ready to go for your youth group—including pledge cards for the participants, posters, "Let It Growl!" buttons and T-shirts, and so on. They will furnish free films and suggest other activities to help make the event a success.

AN OVER-65 PARTY

Have the junior highers throw a party for the senior citizens of the community. Play games, serve refreshments, sing old songs the old-timers know, and do things with them, rather than just having them watch. It makes the old folks feel a little younger, helps the kids to learn to appreciate the elderly, and makes a great service project.

RAKE AND RUN

Here's a great way to involve junior highers in a ministry to the community if you live in a neighborhood with a lot of trees. Load up all the kids in a bus and "arm" each with a lawn rake. Go along streets and whenever you see a lawn that needs raking, everyone jumps out and rakes all the leaves up. No pay is accepted for any of the work. It is all done in the name of Christ. You might find out the names of shut-ins who cannot rake their own lawns. It can be fun and rewarding for the kids. During the winter, kids can shovel snow in the same way. You can call it "Snow and Blow."

ROCKATHON

Here's a fun idea that involves everyone in the group and serves as a great service project, too. It's a twenty-four-hour rockathon. Each participant signs up sponsors for twenty-five cents (or more) for every hour he rocks on his rocking chair. Here are the rules.

1. Everyone provides his own rocking chair.
2. Participants must rock at least four hours in succession.
3. Time breaks allowed only for trips to the bathroom.
4. The chair must be moving at all times.

Hold the event in a large room and supply plenty of TVs, record players, radios, coffee, cookies, and lemonade. Keep the participants awake by cheering, and a lot of cold, wet towels. Meals can be provided by the church or families.

After participants finish rocking, they are given an official time certificate to show their sponsor. Keep a master record of all participants and their times to make sure each sponsor's money is collected. Take a lot of pictures, advertise it well in advance, and invite spectators. Also, keep track of the total amount of money raised and announce it to the kids every four or five hours. It keeps enthusiasm high. The money can then be donated to a worthy cause of the group's choosing.

SCAVENGER FOOD HUNT

This game is fun, and it can also make a significant contribution to a poor family or families in your local area, especially around Thanksgiving. The group is divided into teams and is given a list of canned goods or other food items they are to collect from homes within a specified area. Whichever group collects the most items on the list is the winner, but the real winners are the people who receive the donated food. Each home that contributes should receive a thank-you note, which can also serve as a receipt. It is best to work through a local welfare agency or other organization that can help with the distribution of the food.

THE SUPERMARKET BLITZ

Here's another way to collect food for needy families. Station a small group of kids outside the entrances to supermarkets in the area. Be sure to get permission first. The kids should have large containers in which canned goods or other food items can be deposited. They ask people going into the store if they would purchase one extra item of their choice to be donated to a needy family in the area. Make sure the people know that a legitimate church or other agency is involved in the food distribution program, and give receipts to those who desire them. It's a pretty effective way to collect food and to help others in Christ's name.

Notes

CHAPTER ONE

1. Donald A. Wells, "The Educational Plight of the Early Adolescent," unpublished manuscript, 1976. Used by permission.
2. Erik Erikson, *Identity, Youth and Crisis* (New York: W. W. Norton, 1968) p. 91.
3. Ibid., p. 23.
4. Jerome Kagan, "A Conception of Early Adolescence," *Twelve to Sixteen: Early Adolescence*, ed. Robert Coles, et al. (New York: W. W. Norton, 1972), p. 94.
5. Search Institute, "Young Adolescents and Their Parents," *Project Report* (Minneapolis: Search Institute, 1984), p. 12.
6. Erikson, *Identity, Youth and Crisis*, p. 54.
7. "Options in Education," program #95: *Portrait of American Adolescence* (Washingtion: National Public Radio, 1979).
8. Gary Downing, Dr., "Is There Life After Confirmation?" unpublished manuscript, 1985.

CHAPTER TWO

1. Edward Martin, "The Early Adolescent in School," *Twelve to Sixteen: Early Adolescence*, ed. Robert Coles, et al. (New York: W. W. Norton, 1972), p. 193.
2. John A. Rice, *I Came Out of the Eighteenth Century* (New York: Harper & Bros., 1942).
3. Search Institute, "Young Adolescents and Their Parents," p. 97.
4. H. Stephen Glenn, M.D., *Developing Capable Young People* (Hurst, Texas: Humansphere, Inc., 1983). Sound recording.

CHAPTER THREE

1. Wells, "The Educational Plight."
2. James M. Tanner, "Sequence and Tempo in the Somatic Changes in Puberty," *The Control of the Onset of Puberty*, ed. Melvin M. Grumback, Gilman D. Grave, and

Florence S. Mayer (New York: John Wiley and Sons, 1974), p. 455.

3. Joan Lipsitz, "The Age Group," *Toward Adolescence: The Middle School Years,* ed. Maurice Johnson (Chicago: University of Chicago Press, 1980), p. 21.

4. Ibid., p. 21.

CHAPTER FOUR

1. Gilman D. Grave, *The Control of the Onset of Puberty* (New York: John Wiley & Sons, 1974), p. xxiii.

2. Ibid., p. 409.

3. J. M. Tanner, "Sequence, Tempo, and Individual Variation," in *Twelve to Sixteen, Early Adolescence,* ed. Robert Coles, et al. (New York: W. W. Norton, 1972), p. 22.

4. David Bromberg, Stephen Commins, and Stanford B. Friedman, "Protecting Physical and Mental Health," *Toward Adolescence: The Middle School Years,* ed. Maurice Johnson (Chicago: University of Chicago Press, 1980), p. 140.

5. Eric W. Johnson, *How to Live Through Junior High School* (Philadelphia and New York: J. B. Lippincott Co., 1975), p. 39.

6. Quoted in David Elkind, *All Grown Up and No Place to Go* (Reading, Mass.: Addison-Wesley Publishing Co.), p. 49.

7. Search Institute, "Young Adolescents and Their Parents," p. 101. See also J. Norman and M. Harris, *The Private Life of the American Teenager* (New York: Rawson-Wade, 1981).

8. Robert Coles and Geoffrey Stokes, *Sex and the American Teenager* (New York: Harper and Row, 1985), p. 2.

9. Judy Blume, *Letters to Judy* (New York: G. P. Putnam's Sons, 1986), p. 166.

10. Search Institute, "Young Adolescents and Their Parents," p. 88.

11. Mauritz Johnson, ed., *Toward Adolescence: The Middle School Years* (Chicago: University of Chicago Press, 1980), p. 8.

12. Quoted in Coles and Stokes, *Sex and the American Teenager,* p. 2.
13. Coles and Stokes, *Sex and the American Teenager*, p. 38.
14. Search Institute, "Young Adolescents and Their Parents," p. 14.
15. Coles and Stokes, *Sex and the American Teenager*, p. 36.
16. Blume, *Letters to Judy*, p. 155.
17. Coles and Stokes, *Sex and the American Teenager*, p. 47.
18. One example is the curriculum *There is a Season: Studies in Human Sexuality for Youth of Christian Churches and Their Parents,* written by Dorothy Williams and published by C. Brown Co., Dubuque, Iowa. Youth Specialties, El Cajon, Calif., has also published several resources for teaching youth about sexuality and values.
19. Joan Lipsitz, *Growing Up Forgotten* (Lexington, Mass.: Lexington Books, 1977), p. 17.

CHAPTER FIVE

1. Joan Lipsitz, *Growing Up Forgotten,* p. 122.
2. Joan Lipsitz, "The Age Group," in *Toward Adolescence: The Middle School Years,* ed. Mauritz Johnson (Chicago: The National Society for the Study of Education), p. 14.
3. Alvin W. Howard and George C. Stoumbis, *The Junior High and Middle School: Issues and Practices* (Scranton, Pa.: Intext Educational Publishers, 1970), p. 34. Used by permission of Harper and Row Publishers, Inc.
4. Jerome Kagan, "A Conception of Early Adolescence," p. 103.
5. R. D. Enright, D. K. Lapsley, and L. M. Olsen, "Early Adolescent Labor" *The Journal of Early Adolescence* 5, no. 4 (Winter, 1985), pp. 402–403.
6. David Elkind, *All Grown Up and No Place To Go*, pp. 4–5.
7. Search Institute, "Young Adolescents and their Parents," pp. 50–55.
8. Eda J. Le Shan, *Sex and Your Teenager: A Guide for Parents* (New York: David McKay Co., 1969), p. 51. Used by permission.

9. Eric W. Johnson, *How to Live Through Junior High School,* p. 199.

CHAPTER SIX

1. For more information on this theory see Herman Epstein, "Growth Spurts During Brain Development: Implications for Educational Policy" (chapter 10), *Education and the Brain,* ed. J. Chall (Chicago: National Society for the Study of Education Yearbook, University of Chicago Press, 1979). Also see Conrad F. Toepfer, Jr., "Brain Growth Periodization—A New Dogma for Education?" *The Middle School Journal* (August, 1979).
2. Hershel Thornburg, editor of *The Journal of Early Adolescence* (University of Arizona). Letter to author 13 April 1983. "Developmental psychologists as a whole believe that brain growth periodization has no validity at all. . . . In short, I believe the theory has little or nothing to offer our understanding of adolescent thought."
3. Kohlberg and Carol Gilligan, "The Adolescent as Philosopher," *Twelve to Sixteen: Early Adolescence,* ed. Robert Coles, et al. (New York: W. W. Norton, 1972), p. 154.
4. David Elkind, *All Grown Up and No Place to Go,* p. 24.
5. Eric W. Johnson, *How To Live Through Junior High School,* p. 34.
6. Quoted in Joan Lipsitz, *Growing Up Forgotten,* p. 47.
7. Jerome Kagan, "A Conception of Early Adolescence," pp. 93–94.
8. Lipsitz, *Growing Up Forgotten,* p. 47.

CHAPTER SEVEN

1. David Breskin, "Dear Mom and Dad," *Rolling Stone Magazine,* No. 434 (November 8, 1984): 26.
2. David Elkind, "Understanding the Young Adolescent," *Adolescence,* XIII, No. 49 (Spring 1978): 127–134.
3. Delia Ephron, *Teenage Romance* (New York: Viking Press, 1981), p. 37.
4. Elkind, *All Grown Up and No Place to Go,* p. 38.

5. Bill Wennerholm, "Adolescence, the Bridge from Self-Esteem to Self-Esteem," *Changes* 1, No. 1 (Spring 1982): 3.
6. Search Institute, "Young Adolescents and Their Parents," p. 129.
7. Leah M. Lefstein and William Kerewsky, *3:00 to 6:00 P.M.: Young Adolescents at Home and in the Community* (Carrboro, North Carolina: The Center for Early Adolescence, 1982), p 2.
8. *Youth Report* (New York: Grafton Publications, January 1976): p. B1.

CHAPTER EIGHT

1. Frederick Buechner, *Wishful Thinking* (New York: Harper and Row, 1973), p. 20.
2. Elkind, *All Grown Up and No Place to Go*, p. 42.
3. Search Institute, "Young Adolescents and Their Parents," p. 160.
4. Elkind, *All Grown Up and No Place to Go*, p. 43.
5. Ibid., p. 40.
6. Alvin W. Howard and George C. Stoumbis, *The Junior High and Middle School: Issues and Practices*, p. 34.
7. Bruno Bettelheim, quoted in "Reflections," *Christianity Today*, Volume 25, No. 5, p. 47.

CHAPTER NINE

1. Gayle Dorman and Joan Lipsitz, "Early Adolescent Development," *Middle Grades Assessment Program: User's Manual* (Chapel Hill, North Carolina: Center for Early Adolescence, 1981), pp. 6–8.